Mental Makeover
Reclaiming Your Beauty from the Inside Out

Thank you for sharing your story!

Sharonda N. Stiggers

Sharonda Stiggers, CFLE-P

Sharonda Stiggers
P.O. Box 2241
Cleveland, TN 37320-2241
info@sharondastiggers.com
Sharondastiggers.com

Limits of Liability and Disclaimer of Warranty
The author and publisher shall not be liable for your misuse of this material. This book is strictly for informational and educational purposes.
Warning – Disclaimer
The purpose of this book is to educate and entertain. The author and/or publisher do not guarantee that anyone following these techniques, suggestions, tips, ideas, or strategies will become successful. The author and/or publisher shall have neither liability nor responsibility to anyone with respect to any loss or damage caused, or alleged to be caused, directly or indirectly by the information contained in this book.
All scripture quotations are taken from the King James Version of the Bible.

ISBN 9781941749579
Library of Congress Catalog Number 2016911779

Edited by: Shavonna Bush
Cover Design: Kingdom Graphica
Interior Design: Laura Brown

4-P Publishing
Chattanooga, TN

Contact Sharonda

To contact Sharonda Stiggers for speaking engagements and other business please send an email to info@sharondastiggers.com

For words of encouragement, continued offers, virtual discussions, and much more subscribe to: www.sharondastiggers.com to hear more from the author.

"Like" Sharonda Stiggers' Books on Facebook for quick updates, and weekly motivation!

Stay connected with Sharonda! For business, social inquiries, or more information connect via email, Facebook and Instagram!

Dedication

To my mother, you are my angel on earth. Without your divine love, I would not be the woman I am today. Your counsel, prayer, and wisdom have given me the confidence and strength necessary to live out my dreams. Thank you for the constant support and encouragement. You have shown me what it is to navigate life with the might of a lion, and the heart of a dove.

Acknowledgements

Thank you Shavonna Bush, with the writing of this book I have gained not only a friend but also the big sister that I never had. Throughout this process, you have mentored me both personally and professionally. Thank you for introducing me to S.W.A.T., which has been one of the greatest blessings to come into my life. You have helped me make my dreams come true! I hope to be as good of a friend to you as you have been to me. I love you dearly.

Mrs. Laura Brown, or as I like to call you, "Coach Laura," thank you for creating S.W.A.T. Book Camp for authors. You have provided a platform for authors to be a ministry to those who need them; that is powerful.

My wonderful "sister" Camille Farmer, thank you for always bringing my vision to life with your awesome photography! Your patience, professionalism, and poise have taken you so far. I'm proud to have you in my life.

Marcus McDonald, my brother and one and only sibling. I love you and thank you for the advice and tough love. Thank you for being the first person I looked up to. You are my role model.

Christine Turner and Karla Scaife, thank you both for being my beta readers and giving your input! You both are extremely busy, and it meant so much to me to hear what you had to say regarding my work. I love you both dearly.

Seven, the artist, I am very happy to have worked with you. I have admired your art around the city of Chattanooga, and I am honored to work with such a talented, kind, and patient artist, directly from my birth city. Thank you for helping to make my vision a reality!

Mr. and Mrs. Pickeral, I am so glad God brought you two wonderful people into my life. Mr. Pickeral, thank you for sharing your talents with me and creating an amazing website.

To my supportive friends, Shianne Williams, Courtnay Moon, Kayla Banes, Allison Whitmore, and Jearea Morrison, thank you, ladies, for being there for me when I needed a listening ear, advice, or just a good laugh. I love you all!

Last, but certainly not least, I want to give honor to My Lord and Savior Jesus Christ. Without you, I would not have made it this far. You have given me the strength that I did not know I had to serve you in this special way. Thank you, Lord, for loving me with no end.

About the Author

Sharonda Stiggers is a native of Cleveland, TN. She was born in the neighboring city of Chattanooga and enjoys serving both communities. She also lived in Columbia, SC and Syracuse, NY. She currently resides in her hometown of Cleveland.

Education has always been a passion for Sharonda. She received her Bachelors of Science in Child Development and Family Studies, in addition to her minor in Business Administration from Middle Tennessee State University. She is also a Certified Family Life Educator. She began serving as a mentor to inner city youth during her undergraduate studies, and continues to do so within her own community. Her love for education and heart for those in need shone brightly as she began her adult life and tapped into her potential. Sharonda is an advocate for mental health, speaker, and youth mentor.

Through the process of overcoming anxiety, depression and personal hardships, Sharonda has discovered the importance of maintaining a positive and healthy mind-set, "My goal for my readers is for them to know that their minds are very powerful. How you feel on the inside, dictates how you navigate through life on the outside. I want them to know the importance of keeping their mind on Christ. 'Thou wilt keep him in perfect peace, whose mind is stayed on thee: because he trusteth in thee.' (Isaiah 26:3)."

She enjoys blogging, exercising, laughter, and her alone time with The Lord. You can read Sharonda's blogs at Sharondastiggers.com.

Contents

Preface

It's makeover time! No, I will not do your hair. Well, not unless you want me to. I mean I can, but I suggest you see a professional. I'm sorry; I cannot do your makeup. I have just begun to master the art of doing my own! But, if you want me to I can try, and we can cross our fingers and hope for the best. Wardrobe? Let me refer you to an awesome stylist. Wait! Before you turn and walk out of this makeover session, let me assure you, I CAN help.

Take this journey with me, as we will see a transformation. This book is like your "advice in a makeup bag". You are here to receive a "Mental Makeover". This is a renewal of the mind. For me, beauty starts within. I look my best when I am actually at my best mentally and spiritually. Although I can admit, there have been many occasions where I appeared happy, but was under much devastation and spiritual warfare. This is what many people call a "dressed up mess." I do not want this for you. Authentic happiness and peace is our goal. In this book, I will show you how I have gotten from devastation to elevation.

If you have a mirror, take a look, I want you to *genuinely* love and value what you see. Every flaw, blemish, dimple, freckle, crooked tooth or gap, embrace these things, for it does not matter what is on the outside; what really matters is how you feel about yourself on the inside. Say this with me:

"I am not afraid to love who I am, and I accept myself exactly as I am."

I asked you to speak these words simply because words are powerful! 'Death and life are in the power of the tongue: and they that love it shall eat the fruit thereof.' (Proverbs 18:21). Speak life over your situations, and watch your seeds grow. Pretty soon, there will be beautiful flowers, in a once dry wasteland.

Throughout this book, you will find several affirmations. I want you to say them aloud, physically speak life and positivity over yourself. Okay, I understand that blurting out affirmations publicly may gather a few stares, and you may not want to risk the chance of embarrassment. I totally get it. If this is your reservation, bookmark the page, highlight the affirmation, and come back to it in your alone time. But if you are one of those people who do not care, by all means, say it loud and say it proud! I'm with you!

This is your book so do not be afraid to write in it. I have provided journal pages throughout the book as well to give you opportunities to form dialogue with your thoughts. If you are unable to put your thoughts into words, draw those feelings, and express it that way.

While you are reading the compilation of poems and essays within this book, make the necessary connections to your own journey. Whenever these connections are made, apply the takeaways, lessons, and tips to your life. We are no longer allowing negative thoughts to enter our minds and have dominion over our lives.

So now, are you ready for your makeover? Thank you for making the decision to take this journey. I pray that there are breakthroughs, and I pray you find peace here.

Connect with me at info@sharondastiggers.com.

I look forward to hearing from you!

"What's on the outside makes a first impression, but what's on the inside leaves a lasting impression" – Dr. David. L. Banks

Concealer

What are You Hiding?

'Shall not God search this out? For he knoweth the secrets of the heart.' (Psalm 44:21)

So it's 6 p.m., and you are contemplating your attendance to a girl's night out that you previously committed to. Three of your closest friends will be there, in addition to that one not so close friend; you know the one in which you often need to put on the happy face for whenever they're around, but your dear friends just don't get it... yes that one!

Anyway, you're cringing with regret because you would much rather stay in. Oh, and remember that happy face? Guess what? You've got a visitor, Mr. Pimple! So you might add a little concealer, maybe even some foundation to that happy face. A dab here, a tad there.... *aah* your masterpiece is complete. Since Mr. Pimple is partying with you tonight and maybe even tomorrow night, it's best we cover him. We do not know the length of his residency, but one thing's for sure, he is unwanted; kind of like that friend you'd prefer stay home!

I want us to take a closer look at the beauty product concealer for what it is and what it does. For those of you who do not know, concealer is a flesh-toned cosmetic item; designed with an intention to cover blemishes or dark areas on the face. When used appropriately, a girl can work miracles in this step of the makeup routine. Trust me, I know!

Now typically when I do my makeup, I can be seen jamming out to my favorite tunes while putting on a show in the mirror. However, there are often times when I appreciate tranquility and relish in the delight of listening to my thoughts in solitude. I remember standing at my vanity taking careful strokes to my forehead and cheekbones while pondering over the idea of purpose. Everyone and everything has a purpose. Teachers are meant to educate, doctors are here to heal us, and concealer... well... it hides stuff! Unpleasant areas are covered up, and are temporarily "non-existent". How powerful is that?

While it may be impressive in its function, the idea of masking imperfections can be quite unhealthy in theory. Making the conscious decision to avoid what pains you instead of acknowledging and approaching these challenges head on, is only a temporary fix. Think of it in relation to our existence. How often do you find yourself hiding or denying imperfect segments of your life, and exactly how effective has this been?

If you do not see it, does that mean it no longer exists? Just like a breakout or blemish, covering up a situation does not eliminate it, so why hide it? With the power of makeup, one is equipped with the ability to trick others (and maybe even ourselves momentarily) that our complexion is blemish-free, but as soon as we come home, and remove our masks, we see it; we see the imperfections. The makeup was nothing more than a temporary fix to a problem that involves a bit more work.

Now, do not get me wrong, I absolutely love makeup, and I am all for enhancing beauty. However, before you put on all this glory, there is a cleaning process you should go through. So just like you should cleanse your face before applying your makeup, there should also be a cleansing and a renewal of the mind that takes place in order to effectively take on the world. We want to cleanse our minds of negativity, self-doubt, fears, and anything that causes mental strain or distraction. As you continue reading, each chapter will give you some tools to help you with this cleansing.

Remember; love the skin you're in, even if it isn't flawless. We are beautiful products of God's creation, with or without makeup. I really hope you feel the same way. So, please join me in this declaration:

"I am beautiful, just the way I am."

You are beautiful just as you are. God took his time with you. He created you in a very special way, and with purpose! We are His clay, and God is the potter. Remember that!

The metaphors I am using in this chapter and throughout the book are comparisons to various beauty items you may see on any woman's vanity table, in relation to various topics and occurrences we experience in real life. Just like concealer covers things, so did I. It was much easier for me to hide what I was feeling, instead of being open and present with those emotions.

Another defense mechanism for me was avoidance. Averting deep-rooted pain from my past, and running from my emotions, personal secrets, or even the way I felt about a person or a specific situation was the best way for me to cope. This was a safe place for me. Unfortunately, this did more harm than good. Before I knew it, the things I ran from made an encore appearance back into my thoughts, and I knew it was time to release them.

Eventually, we all reach a point in time in which we have to deal with the things we tuck away. You may feel inclined to continue avoiding or prolonging these issues, but don't do it! If you can think of a few situations that have caused you consistent distress, or if one major instance is screaming out at you, it is now the time to take action.

Once you acknowledge its existence, and you have admitted to yourself that this is an aspect of your life, the next step is to seek comfort in the Lord and ask of Him what you need. Whether it is help, healing, direction, peace, etc. it is vital that you take your problems to God; He will set you free. He wants us to heal of this mental bondage. You don't have to live as though these things do not exist.

There is an inner sense of negativity and shame that can come as a result of "concealing" displeasing areas of our lives. The more we hide and the more we deny, the more shame we feel. Even though life's misfortunes are uncomfortable to relive, one should not feel ashamed of any aspect of their journey. All of our experiences are essential elements of our story. Each page in your book matters!

Think of it this way, if your life were a book, and you decided to rip out the mortifying or uncomfortable pages of your nonfiction masterpiece, would it still make sense to your reader? Most importantly, would it make sense to the author? Making the decision to actively acknowledge every "page" or aspect of your life, good or bad, allows you to better understand who you are, how you operate, and why. There is a clear storyline, it is authentic, and it is beautiful. The good thing about books, they get better as you read them! With each page, the story grows and develops, just like you!

Additionally, you may often come across people that will need you to be transparent with them. Those concealed occurrences in your life may be what someone needs to hear in order to gain necessary insight into their own lives. We go through things to learn from them, and in turn, help others. Pouring into others so that we may be blessed. You may be the answer to someone's question. Be a blessing to someone by sharing the knowledge gained from your lessons learned!

Those painful truths or "skeletons in your closet", have contributed to you in some way. Through hardship, you have gained much more than you have lost. Any occurrence, whether positive or negative, is conducive to your growth. Therefore, it is best to embrace life's fortunes, and also its misfortunes because at the end of the day, you are an overcomer, and you will overcome! So, if you are currently in or are reflecting upon a dark season in your life, breathe, pray, and know that it will be okay. Begin to come to a realization that there is a lesson to be learned in these situations.

After acknowledging what has been deeply rooted within you, don't go back. Keep pushing forward. This is the beginning of your healing process.

Mirror Moment

What have I been hiding from myself?
Draw or write your emotions as you come clean.

Embrace Your Scars

To protect my emotions, I concealed my scars

Which resulted in an array of self-doubt

And without those feelings out on display,

There was much less to grow anxious about

But I've learned that scars have voices

Because I've heard mine screaming out loud

In life, we are given two choices,

To live bold and fearless, or timid and head bowed

Healing those scars called for transparency

And acceptance for all things real

Shame will no longer be associated with my scars

With time and love they'll heal

"Always remember you are braver than you believe, stronger than you seem, and smarter than you think."
-Christopher Robin

Depression

"The opposite of depression is not happiness, but vitality, and it was the vitality that seemed to seep away from me in that moment."
-Andrew Solomon

Perhaps the exhaustion stemmed from the sheer fact that I was withholding this secret. If not the secret, maybe it was my own self-inflicted verbal abuse. Was the cause of my daunting fatigue the negative and delusionary speaking cycling over and over throughout my mind? Either way, it all began with me. I was the source of the issue that hung over me. So does this mean that it was entirely my fault?

Days quickly turn into nights and back into days again. This is happening all around you, independently and without your help. You did not wake up and declare it was morning, the birds sang, and the sun arose without waiting for you. Then the hand on the clock spun as the hours passed, and you did not care. The only thing that caught you by surprise was how quickly the night fell. The time between the sun and the moon is spent with delusional thoughts that have become a reality for you. From my perspective, this is but a glimpse into that dispirited reality.

What have I hidden? What was concealed? What is it that I did not want people to know? Total despondency. This was a rather personal segment of my life that I shared only with my mother, father, brother, and possibly a close friend or two.

Shame was not the cause of concealing my de-presssssion. That was not my reason for hiding this. Instead, I felt like a burden, not to just to anyone, but to everyone, even myself. Dealing with these emotions alone was much easier. Therefore, this was often a time of seclusion for me, and I decided to deal with my emotions independently.

I have supportive friends, so I knew that by disclosing my depression to them, they would be checking on me every day or even every few hours. I could not handle that. I barely wanted to talk or click the channel button on the remote, how am I supposed to check in with my friends? Fake the funk, for 200 Alex? I think so.

When you think of the definition of a supermom, my mother takes the cake. She is very involved and invested in my life. When it comes to my feelings, her concern goes a step further. She takes on my emotions. When I'm upset, she's upset. Of course, I do not want her to carry this type of agony, so I resisted burdening her with my issues. I came to the conclusion that it would be best to deal with this on my own. I tried to hide it from her and everyone else whenever possible.

I hated the fact that I let life get me down. I would think, "What a waste of a life you are!" I wanted to live freely like everyone else my age! Instead, I felt trapped inside my thoughts. I was a prisoner to my mind. I did not understand how I could quickly go from vibrantly loving life with passion and vitality to despising every aspect of life.

I would question why things impacted me so heavily. It bothered me that other people also had hard times, and they seemed to deal with life in a much healthier way. Now as I look back on that very thought, the reality is, those people possibly could have been hiding their depression just as well as I was.

If you experience any form of depression, please seek the proper help you need. In my experience, wrestling with those emotions in solitude is much more challenging. If you do not know where to begin, simply start by telling someone you trust, such as your mom or your best friend. Whoever it is, be sure to have confidence in the person's ability to handle this with delicacy. This is a sensitive time that should be treated with love and compassion.

Because depression is a word used so inter-changeably, it is much harder to determine how severe someone may be hurting. We live in an era where it is "depressing" to have overslept for class. Or it may be "depressing" that you can't afford concert tickets to your favorite singer's next show. However, the actual state of depression is more complicated than this.

Depression is a state of drudgery, confusion, self-doubt, lack of interest, feelings of worthlessness, and other related conditions. Often it is even a lack of self-care. It may be too much of a chore to get up, shower, and handle your daily hygiene needs. "I'm not going anywhere today, I don't need to get up." I remember a particular time in college when I was going through this, and it physically hurt my body to move. On the flipside, there were days when the only physical activity I did was take care of my hygiene then immediately slump right back into my misery.

The thought of even checking email or handling daily responsibilities may cause some anxious feelings. Depression is more than a momentary sense of sadness. Those who experience depression are unsure of its expiration date or if it even has one. Our everyday moods can be modified, however, major depression is not as easily adjusted.

It did not take very much for me to reach a depressed state. What worried me most was the fact that I never knew what could trigger it. In most cases, it came out of nowhere. As I reflect now, I have found that it was often due to a number of things that I held in. It was a snowball effect. For example, if things went rough for weeks at a time, then by week four, I would more than likely be drained. Sometimes, I would still be processing or healing from something that happened in the past. The avoidance usually resonated, and those feelings I ran from came to the surface.

I consider myself a strong person, so it was difficult to understand why and how I often ended up in this miserable state. Pretty soon the frustration was not only a direct result of the depression, but it was with myself. My attempt to "be strong" caused me to downplay the sadness that I was feeling in order to stay productive and passionate in my daily life. Undervaluing those emotions, only built them up, depression was usually the likely outcome. This was a disappointment, because now my personal strength is in question, although it was my strength that got me here.

As I think back to my senior year in college, it all makes sense. I know that I am not alone when I say senior year is a struggle! Left and right, I was being hit with stumbling blocks. The scariest part was when I did not think I would graduate on time because I signed up for the wrong class. Yes, the wrong class!

I was a Business Administration minor, so I only needed to take the Intro to Accounting course. Well, to my surprise I was about three weeks into Accounting I, the real deal, and boy was I in over my head. The lecture was like a foreign language to me! I began to wonder, "How in the world was I going to pass this test within a week?" What a mess! Thankfully, after several sleepless nights, phone calls, and pleas, I was able to switch out of the class. I was even given a partial refund back for enrollment, and things seemed to be falling into place. However, this was only the tip of the iceberg.

In the summer of 2014, I lost my grandmother to lung cancer. I miss her dearly. This was one of the most painful losses that I have experienced thus far. We were extremely close. She always rooted for me to be the absolute best that I could be. All I wanted was for her live to see me accomplish my dream and graduate from college, and it had been on my mind that entire year that she would not be there to celebrate with me. It pained me to know that I would not be able to run to her after the ceremony clasping my cap to my head with one hand, and holding my degree with the other. Nevertheless, I know she left this world with all confidence that I would make this dream a reality, and I did.

I also struggled with the abandoned emotions of a previous relationship. My first love and first real boyfriend of many, many years have never left my thoughts. We separated midway through my undergraduate year, but I never stopped thinking about him. It did not help that he and I were still romantically and emotionally involved. There was so much confusion there. I begged God for answers, "do you want me to be with him or do you want us to part ways?" I was confused. The only thing that I was sure of was that I loved him.

In my mind, my personal problems were only distractions. So I needed to distract myself from these personal "distractions" and maximize my potential. This was all the more reason for me to throw myself into my classwork, organizations, and occupations. Yes, occupations, plural. At this point, I was in school full-time, working two part-time jobs, was an intern, and a member of about three or four organizations. Somewhere in that schedule I ate and made it to organization meetings. There were sacrifices. Sometimes I was late for commitments and other times I did not show up at all because I was triple and quadruple booked for everything.

Due to this hectic schedule, by Friday I was spent. Outside interaction with others was too much of a task. I just needed my alone time. Many of these days were involved with plenty of wine! I can laugh about this now, but the reality of it all is, this is not the way to handle stress. Being overwhelmed should not be a free pass to drink, and self-medicating on the weekends is not a practical or productive solution. Because guess what? This is another one of those "temporary fixes". I know what you're thinking, "this behavior is normal for the typical college student!" Well, in my alone time I did not do this for fun and social moments, I did it to cope and to escape my reality.

The decision to be "strong" and avoid what pained me, instead of acknowledging my feelings head on, wore me completely out both mentally and physically. I made the mistake of viewing avoidance as strength. In reality, sadness and anxious feelings have the ability to resurface at any given time, especially when avoided or un-resolved. In my world, I had so many other things to have concern for, such as my studies and my future career plans. I took full advantage of this notion and left my emotional life hanging in the balance. I eventually slid into several occasions of depression.

If you can relate, and have experienced instances of depression, there are a few things you should know

You are NOT alone

You have a Heavenly Father who is there with you every step of the way. 'Nevertheless I am continually with thee: thou hast holden me by my right hand.' (Psalm 73:23) 'Be strong and of good courage, fear not, nor be afraid of them: for the Lord thy God, he it is that doth go with thee; he will not fail thee, nor forsake thee.' (Deuteronomy 31:6).

You are also not alone in what you feel. Many people across the globe are suffering. Unfortunately, it is something most of us hide. According to World Health Organization, more than 350 million people have depression globally. Because of the stigma associated with depression and other related mental health disorders, many people fail to acknowledge what they are going through and do not seek treatment, which brings me to my next point.

Do not deny your experience

What is the technique of resilience? Honesty. Be forthright with the fact that you have had or are having this experience. This is how you achieve resilience, and ultimately survival.

Please do not deny what you are feeling. Pay attention to your emotions. Do not overlook the seriousness of spending countless days shutting out the world, while contemplating ways to end your life. Do not ignore that feeling of hopelessness or lack of purpose. Do not make light of that consistent sadness that threw countless wedges into your plans. Instead, take the depression seriously, because it is, in fact, a very serious matter! Acknowledging this will bring a much needed realistic perspective to your condition. "Shutting out the depression strengthens it; while you hide from it, it grows." – Andrew Solomon

You WILL get through this!

Know that you are more than a conqueror, and you will get through this! 'Nay, in all these things we are more than conquerors through him that loved us.' (Romans 8:37) You may not feel that power right now, but it is in you!

If you are wondering how to get through depression or severe sadness, you should first know that you have the power to overcome this obstacle. The next step is assuring you have the necessary support system to back you through this. You are going to need help. The number one source of help comes from the Most High.

'I will lift up mine eyes unto the hills,
from whence cometh my help.
My help cometh from the Lord,
which made heaven and earth.
He will not suffer thy foot to be moved
he that keepeth thee will not slumber.
Behold, he that keepeth Israel
shall neither slumber nor sleep.
The Lord is thy keeper
the Lord is thy shade upon thy right hand.
The sun shall not smite thee by day,
nor the moon by night.
The Lord shall preserve thee from all evil
he shall preserve thy soul.
The Lord shall preserve thy going out
and thy coming in
from this time forth,
and even for evermore.'
(Psalm 121: 1-8)

Look to the Lord for help with this situation. He is a savior and a redeemer. Pray and be specific in your prayers regarding your current needs. If you need peace as you are among stressful times, ask for peace. If you are lacking direction and are unsure of which route to take, ask for direction. Seek Him and He will give you the strength necessary to navigate through this dark time. It all seems very cloudy right now, but the rain will clear, and the skies will blue again, just for you.

As I have said previously, talk with someone you trust. Let them know what you are going through. Do not carry the weight alone. You do not have to. If the depression persists, and you feel it necessary to seek professional help, please do so. There are counselors and mental health professionals out there to help you. If you are currently at a university or learning institution, you may want to research the available counseling services offered. My undergraduate institution provided counseling for all students enrolled.

You may also seek counseling within the church. This is the option that I chose to take. In my experience, the church has always been a source of spiritual and mental counsel with consistent positive results. Again, this is my personal experience, things may work differently for you.

There are leaders within the church that are there to help. I have been blessed with two amazing church families that have always been very down to earth in their approach to me. They have sat and spoken powerful words of life over my situations when I had no strength to talk. They have listened to me when all I needed was a listening ear to voice my thoughts. Sometimes all you need is a listening ear. Even though this was the best option for me, I still advise you do what is best for you. Try a few different options! The most important thing is that you are trying.

Another thing that has been helpful for me during times of unhappiness is positive self-talk. That voice inside your head has more power than you think! It has a significant influence on who you are, how you view yourself, and your quality of life. When you are going through severe sadness, that voice is very active. For me, it was usually one of the following:

- "Why do these things happen to me?"
- "I could be doing so much more with my life."
- "I'm not good enough."

These negative statements carry no truth or advancement for you.

However, when we consistently use positive self-talk, we can negate those offensive statements. Take a look at example statements for positive self-talk:

- "I will grow so much from these learning situations!"
- "I have accomplished so much so far!"
- "I am more than enough!"

Positive self-talk gives you hope, strength, and vitality. The negative statements just weigh you down and leave you hopeless. I know it seems hard to speak positively when you don't feel positive, but do it anyway! It will eventually be something you automatically do. Using myself as an example, when I feel like the negative statement, "I could be doing so much more with my life," I always try to follow that thought with, a "but." "But, I have strong faith." "But I have defeated the odds." "But, I am still alive and have a work to do on earth." "But, I have my health." Or "But I accomplished my dream, and graduated college." Whatever your "But" is, use it! This allows you to focus on those gratifying moments. These are the moments we should be thankful for. Fight off those negative voices!

If you are a visual person, you may need to physically see these positive mantras. Try sticking some post-it notes in areas that you will easily see them. I had a friend who placed notes around her bathroom mirror. The mirror is a great spot to put them because you'll see them each morning as you're getting ready to start your day! You can post your words of empowerment anywhere. I've even made positive notes for myself and stuck them in my planner on days that I knew I'd need to see them, such as a test day or an upcoming interview! Whatever works for you, go for it! Be sure to remain consistent in your positive self-talk. Wake up and declare an uplifting statement on your behalf. Make this statement the standard for your day. Tomorrow, try a different one. Talk yourself through this difficult time, you will get through this! Here is an example of a mantra to declare at the start of your day:

"Today I will allow only positive thoughts to enter my mind."

The greatest nugget to gain here is the aspect of time. Immediate attention can shorten the life of a potential long-term problem. You may think that putting off seeking help for your depression is a likely option because it, "eventually just goes away." However, how much time will you allow? Will you allow days, weeks, months, or even a year or more? How much time will you let escape you, and exactly how long will you let this state of sorrow have dominion over your life? I am reminded of a depressed seventeen-year-old. So many nights I spent silent and in the dark when I should have been out enjoying life! How old are you? How many times will you be that age again?

Of course, life gets you down, but we only get one shot at this. Live it to the fullest! Hug your mother tighter. Call your friends more and let them know what they mean to you, and allow twice as much time for self-care.

Lastly, it is important to value your experience. Begin to search within yourself, and gather what you have learned from the depression. Using myself as an example: I am incredibly thankful that these experiences have taught me to lean on the Lord. I have learned how reflective I am. I have learned that my reflective thoughts can turn into negative ones, and to be mindful of the nature of my speaking.

"I am in full control of my thoughts and emotions, and I will overcome this obstacle."

Depression "Makeup Tips"

💋 Jesus loves you! Remember, 'For God so loved the world that he gave his only begotten Son, that whoever believeth in him should not perish, but have everlasting life.' (John 3:16)

💋 You don't have to take on your burdens alone. Pray and ask God for help with whatever is troubling you. Once you have prayed, trust that it will be taken care of, and be of good courage.

💋 Create for yourself a solid support system, and surround yourself with love.

💋 Engage in positive self-talk throughout the day.

Mirror Moment

At the onset of depression, what are ways that I will combat it?

Suppression or Repression?

Suppression

- an act or instance of suppressing: the state of being suppressed
- the conscious intentional exclusion from the consciousness of a thought or feeling
  -Merriam-Webster's Dictionary

Repression

the act of not allowing a memory, feeling, or desire to be expressed
-Merriam-Webster's Dictionary

Repression, in psychoanalytic theory, the exclusion of distressing memories, thoughts, or feelings from the conscious mind.
-Brittanica.com

It was not until college that I realized I had a serious problem. It was my junior year, to be exact. I was unaware that for the majority of my young adult life I had been carrying such a heavy burden. Suppression was the silent villain of my fortitude. The scary part is, I had no clue.

I attended an event with a friend of mine, representing our undergraduate organization. In my mind, I am just here supporting another great organization and a worthy cause. For me, it was no different from any other day, or any other college event for that matter. Boy, was I in for a surprise.

This all-girl function covered various topics that women often encounter within our life's journey. Most all of these topics were pretty heavy, and I could feel that this was not just going to be your ordinary event. My suspicions did not fail me.

At the start of the gathering, we all got acquainted with one another and began our introductions, which included our name, major, and an interesting or quirky fact about ourselves. We grew comfortable with each other quickly and shared many laughs. I am reminded of a moment when one of the attendants showed off her interesting fact by blurting out, "My name is _____. I am from _____. My major is _____, and I am double-jointed!" and quickly shifted her arms into a seemingly uncomfortable stretch. Laughs were exchanged, and the tension finally lifted.

After the introductions, we began our discussion and exchange of ideas. The topics grew heavier with each moment. Pretty soon, our playful exteriors vanished, and I knew the energy in the room would shift once again. This time, it was a feeling of transparency which happens to be my personal favorite. One by one, young women shared their heart-wrenching truths. It seemed as though each story shared grew heavier and heavier with each breath taken. I was impressed by their braveness. With the strength of a lion, my peers expressed and exposed the pieces of their heart. The transparency of each woman was as real and as raw as a well-written poem. It was beautiful.

Confessions of depression, low self-esteem, familial strains, and abusive relationships are all examples of topics in which we exchanged views. Now, the most disturbing part for me regarding this experience is through all the fearless testimonies, I was affected, but I was disconnected.

The disconnection was not purposely done... or was it? How could one be genuinely disconnected to topics like depression, low self-esteem, and abuse when they have experienced all three? How did I sit through all of these stories without connecting in some way?

The turning point for me began with the words shared by my dear friend. She began to speak with a warm smile and a calm disposition, so my initial thoughts were that she was preparing to give a few words of encouragement to the ladies. Many of the young women in the room were underclassmen, so I was under the impression that she was about to share some great advice. I was all ears and excited to hear what she was about to say. Any word of motivation to brighten the mood would be great.

Then, the calm disposition that she had worn so nicely quickly faded. She revealed that she was abused as a child, and instantly burst into tears. It absolutely crushed me, although I wanted to stay strong for her. I kept my composure, embraced her, and praised her for her transparency amongst a room full of women whom we, for the most part, had just met!

During my drive home, I began to reflect over our impactful evening. God began to speak to me; I knew I was supposed to be there, but why exactly? My heart was full, I felt for the ladies, and I was also happy for their strength and courageous transparency. And then it hit me, BAM...what about me?

I had just attended this amazing event but used no form of introspection. Not once did I search within myself to relate with the other ladies. In some strange way, I felt for them and took on their pain, but I did not connect with their experiences. The suppression that I had created for myself after all these years was mighty. Throughout the course of my life, I excluded these feelings to protect myself. This was my defense mechanism, and the seriousness was revealed to me all on this day.

Well, to my memory, at a very young age, I was inappropriately touched. Even now I question if this *really* happened? I was so young and didn't understand much about this, all I knew was that it was wrong. It was not until age twenty-three that I finally decided to express the occurrence to my parents. The weight was finally lifted, but why did I wait so long to speak about it? Well, to be honest, this is not a memory that has always been with me.

As I mentioned previously, my response to the trauma caused the occurrence to be a fading memory for me. According to the American Psychological Association, "Some clinicians theorize that children understand and respond to trauma differently from adults. Some furthermore believe that childhood trauma may lead to problems in memory storage and retrieval." (apa.org) The article also explains that dissociation is a possible justification for a memory that was forgotten and later recalled (apa.org). Dissociation simply means a memory is not actually lost, but unavailable for retrieval for a length of time. This better explains my disconnection with the stories that should have hit home for me at this all-girl event.

As I continued my research, it occurred to me that this memory was not a "suppressed" memory, but a *repressed* memory. When your mind blocks out certain events, these memories are traumatic experiences for you. I had been repressing the unfortunate incident that occurred in my childhood. Repression is the reason why I did not remember this awful experience. The freedom that I feel from letting go of the "secret" that was so deeply hidden in my thoughts was indeed powerful.

If you have gone through a similar experience, you may have experienced either suppression or repression. So let's review, repression is the process of excluding uncomfortable memories, feelings, or thoughts from the conscious mind, ultimately forcing them into the unconscious mind; often causing a lack of awareness or memory lapse for one's own situation. According to Psychology Today, "... the emotion is conscious, but the idea behind it is absent." (psychologytoday.com) This is so true regarding my situation. I always felt this pain, but I hardly made a connection to the details and facts of the occurrence. On the contrary, suppression is the conscious decision to delay unpleasant memories or circumstances. Just think, repression is unconscious, suppression is conscious.

Whether you are suppressing or repressing, it is important to come to grips with those distressing thoughts. The goal is to become in tune with what haunts you and address it. There is freedom in being honest with what you know to be true and all that you feel. I could not connect with the girls at my college event because for years I was unknowingly repressing that dark and confusing time of my life. Your truth is powerful. Just think, because my friend shared her story, I was able to have the epiphany that I was indeed hurting too. There is beauty in transparency and sharing those ugly moments. Our stories may be different, but they are all significant. Sharing those stories carry great impact for both yourself and others.

Why is it important to actively acknowledge suppressed or repressed memories? Well, suppression specifically is generally expected to be ineffective because if you hold back or suppress an emotion, it grows or even worsens. For example, if I was displeased with my brother about a situation but I avoided and held back my emotions, my feelings could eventually turn into anger or hostility.

As for repression, progress is critical. This is for those of you who related to my story. We should be careful not to allow ourselves to travel backward. Once we have gained full access and clarity to the repressed experience or emotion, take power over it. Do not suppress and purposely hold back the feelings of this experience. Take your power back and focus on healing yourself. If you were abused, this may mean talking it out with someone you trust. Or if you are ready, it could even mean staring into the eyes of the abuser and having an honest conversation. This is a decision only you can make. For your next step, seek counsel in order for you to make the best choices necessary for your healing.

Until we stare into the eye of a negative memory, we will always be unavailable. It is unhealthy to be absent within your emotions. This disables the ability to grow and heal authentically. I was unavailable at that all-girl event, and I was also momentarily unavailable for myself.

Once you have acknowledged what you have suppressed or repressed, you will experience the beginning of your healing process. Accepting these experiences may or may not be simple for you. I do know that in my experience, the difficulty came with reliving through what happened and recapping the uncomfortable details that I did not wish to remember. It is quite normal to experience difficulty when trying to recall details of a repressed experience. If this happens, do not fret; the most important part is the acknowledgment.

Stand tall and take charge over whatever you are suppressing or what you have repressed, and use that pain to help others. In my experience, I have found that situations are easy to forget, and extremely difficult to admit. So once you can acknowledge the realness of this occurrence, you have done it! The hard part is over. Most importantly, forgiveness will be key, and an important factor in this healing process. This is where you will begin to experience the closure necessary to move on. No longer will those negative experiences or emotions have power over you.

Mirror Moment

What have I suppressed or repressed?

Your Strength

Your strength is ever-present,

And much larger than your fears

It brings comfort to all things unpleasant

And equips you with the courage to persevere

Your strength can move mountains,

It can calm the unwanted storms

Your strength is a continuous fountain

Flowing, never ending, and greater than the norm

Your strength is a creator

It makes all things anew

No need to search for greater

Your strength lives inside of you

Forgiveness

'For if ye forgive men their trespasses, your heavenly Father will also forgive you, But if ye forgive not men their trespasses, neither will your Father forgive your trespasses.' (Matthew 6:14-15)

'Forbearing one another, and forgiving one another, if any man have a quarrel against any: even as Christ forgave you, so also do ye.' (Colossians 3:13)

If you have ever been hurt or mistreated, whether sexually, verbally, mentally, physically, or emotionally you know forgiveness may not always be the easiest thing to do and I totally understand that! You feel violated, devalued, and depending on where you are in your healing process, you may be bitter. Whoever hurt you had no right to subject you to those feelings. It hurts, and it hurts badly.

I remember the baffling moment just before the first time I learned the value of forgiveness, "I have been mistreated, and you want me to forgive them!?" A question directed towards my mother as she encouraged me to forgive. She quickly answered, "This is not for them. This is for your salvation and self-repair. Jesus wants us to forgive his people." Wow. Seriously guys, it was like my heart had a shield of ice covering it, which immediately melted at that moment. There was no need for further explanation. These are His people. He loves them as He loves us. Through every flaw and mistake, His love is unconditional. We should forgive and love God's people as He loves and forgives us each day. Just as the ice melted off of my heart, so did the anger and frustration. I became overwhelmed with serenity and peace after looking past the flaws of those that hurt me, and simply forgiving them!

As I mentioned in the previous section, forgiveness is the single most important factor in your healing process. There is promise and freedom that comes with letting go of the ill feelings that have once weighed heavily on you. Thinking back to my repressed memory, I needed to forgive the person that harmed me in order to move on from the hurtful and confusing encounter. If I held on to that resentment, the situation would still be current in my life. I will share more about this in the next section.

I don't know about you, but I can only give attention to the things that matter and bring betterment to my life. Make the conscious effort to eliminate all things that are counterproductive to this. If it doesn't bring you any form of increase or positivity, let it go!

Forgiveness is often viewed as a verbal exchange of words. It is associated with one informing the other that, "I forgive you." Although you can do this, it is not necessary. Forgiveness does not call for you to verbalize to those who hurt you that you have forgiven them. Especially if you have been abused or wronged and have not been given any form of apology or amends. Again, the forgiveness is for you. It is the personal decision to forgive and absolve the ill-disposed feelings you once felt that carries the value. As long as there is sincerity in your forgiveness, and you no longer carry resentment, you are well on your way!

If you are holding on to something, I dare you to let go of this pain. This will be the best decision you will make regarding your healing. Forgive and watch the miracles God will work on your behalf.

Forgiveness "Makeup Tips"

💋 Forgiveness is beneficial to your healing process.

💋 You do not have to verbalize to those who hurt you that you have forgiven them.

💋 There is freedom in forgiveness!

💋 The one most positively affected by your forgiveness is you.

Mirror Moment

*I need to forgive*_____

(Insert name)

*for*_____

Truth Hurts

How hurtful is it when you are lied to? How about a little white lie? What if you were lied to over and over again? Frustrating right? At times, the person we lie to is the one in the mirror. The unfortunate thing about this is, whether we realize it or not, we are causing much more agony to ourselves than good. You'll find that it is much better to face reality.

A major reason why we hide certain aspects of our lives is simple... the truth hurts! Sometimes we much rather ignore, act as if these things did not happen, and move on with our lives than to open up those painful wounds. At face value, disregarding painful truths may be how many, "move on" with their lives. However, when you fail to actively acknowledge what pains you the most, you are disabling yourself from engaging in a significant aspect of the healing process.

From experience, I know that it is important to be authentic in all your thoughts. In the truth, you will find comfort. Let's keep this thought in mind- *The better you are real, the more you will be able to deal.* Now, don't get me wrong, I do not want you to dwell on these issues. However, the ultimate goal is self-acceptance. We are accepting the experience while accepting ourselves in the process. I have broken down this concept into a three-step process: recognize, visualize, and verbalize.

The concept behind "recognize, visualize, and verbalize" is acceptance and authenticity. When used in this particular sequence, we can begin to courageously create that bona fide honesty with ourselves. This is an activity that involves action. I know this may feel rather scary but, in the words of Linda Murray Bullard, "Action cures fear," so let's begin!

Recognize

This is the most important step. Have you ever had a day in which you felt down, but you were unsure of the reason? Often, we find ourselves in emotional hardships that are unable to be explained. This could very well be the result of unresolved anger or resentment. Whether it is something we suppressed only a few months ago, from our childhood, or even something frustrating that occurred yesterday and you are just not over it yet; these things resonate with us and affect our lives on a daily basis.

Being transparent and using my experiences as a guide for you- "I recognize that I was violated in my youth. I was very confused by this back then, and I acknowledge the weight this experience has carried. This is a part of my life, and I accept it."

Acknowledge the occurrence, and take power over it. Yes, these things have happened to us, but you do not deserve to let the unfortunate take dominion over your life. Most importantly, God does not want this for you either! 'Cast thy burden upon the Lord, and he shall sustain thee. He shall never suffer the righteous to be moved.' (Psalm 55:22)

Visualize

'Behold, I will do a new thing; now it shall spring forth; shall ye not know it? I will even make a way in the wilderness, and rivers in the desert.' (Isaiah 4319).

God speaks to us here. He wants our faith to have such might that we can actually see Him making a way out of no way. What the Lord can do for us is according to our faith.

I know our pasts and even our recent pains can hurt us, but we should have such trust in the Lord that we can move past what once pained us to no end and become whole again. You may want to visualize yourself healed by Jesus's stripes and strengthened by His power and even using your newfound strength to help others who have also gone through your situation. See yourself in the place you would like to be and then actively apply your faith to this vision.

Ask yourself, "What does it take to get there?" Do you want to tell your story of abuse? Would you like to host speaking engagements at schools or large venues? If you do not have much speaking experience, take baby steps and speak at brunches or small events, then make your way to domestic violence shelters. Believe that you can do this, then step out and actively make the necessary steps to get you there.

Only you and God know the desires of your heart, and it is up to you to make this vision a reality! You may be in a dark season right now, but the important thing to know is that this pain is only temporary. 'For our light affliction, which is but for a moment, worketh for us a far more exceeding and external weight of glory; While we look not at the things which are seen, but at the things which are not seen, for the things which are seen are temporal; but the things which are not seen are eternal.' (2 Corinthians 4:17-18). When I first studied these two verses with understanding, I thought "Wow! So, God, you mean to tell me the occurrences in the physical that I can actually see with my two eyes should not be what I focus on? I only need to believe in your power and abilities, that of which I cannot see?" His answer, "YES!" For example, you may have no form of transportation right now. You can physically look outside and see no vehicle with your name on it. That has no power. This is not your forever. The Lord knows what we need and one day you will be provided this need. Pray and be specific in your prayers, put forth the work, and these things will come to you. In God's perfect timing you will look outside, and there WILL be a vehicle, just for you.

There is power in having revelation of God and his word. According to His word, you will get through your dark times, and you will be provided all that you need. Faith and positive visualization, in conjunction with your work, is an active tool that will help us get there.

Verbalize

"Death and life are in the power of the tongue, and those who love it will eat its fruit" (Proverbs 18:21). We have to remember that our words are powerful! It is extremely important to speak life over your situations. Once again, use my story as a model- "I will no longer carry the hurt or confusion bestowed upon me from the past. It is not my fault, I forgive them, and with my faith and the support of my family... it will not affect my romantic or personal relationships." The positive words you speak over your life will overshadow any doubts or uncertainties that may come your way.

Allowing ourselves the opportunity to be honest about what hurts us is powerful. Even if it seems as though you do not possess the strengths or capabilities, to be honest, you do! Small secrets turn into heavy burdens, and the things we wish to hide can negatively interfere with our growth.

Even though it may feel like we are covering up our issues pretty well, people sense things. The heavier the burden, and the longer it is carried; the more severe it will affect one's quality of life. Most importantly, these internal issues should be rectified within us for our individual health. So, for those hurtful truths that you have carried with you all this time, it is time for healing. Let it go! You do not deserve to carry this any longer. It ends here.

Honesty "Makeup Tips"

- Acknowledging your "painful truths" allow you to take power over them.

- Honesty promotes self-acceptance and personal growth.

- The better you are real, the more you will be able to deal with the unfortunate.

Mirror Moment

What "painful truth" have I struggled with? Draw or write your response.

Perfection

"If everything was perfect, you would never learn and you would never grow." – Beyoncé Knowles

It is not uncommon for you to have a pristine idea of what you think your life should look like; free from error. Although this is customary, aiming for a "perfect life" can cause stress and can often become quite the headache. I know firsthand what it is like to strive for perfection. I also know how upsetting it feels on those occasions of being unsuccessful at reaching a certain level of refinement. If you are a self-proclaimed "perfectionist," I get it. However, I really want you to give yourself a break. It is imperative that you understand that we live in an imperfect world. It is "perfectly" normal to be flawed!

Now, putting this all into perspective, while being introspective, there are a few examples in my life where being the self-proclaimed "perfectionist" has absolutely kicked me in the butt! I remember a young middle-school aged chubby girl entering the sixth grade, who was now a new member of the school concert band.

We moved back to my birth state, Tennessee, after moving to New York while I was in grade school. I remember very clearly my life growing up in Tennessee. I loved my school, adored my friends, and lived a carefree life.

We lived in a nice neighborhood. It was just my mom, dad, brother, myself, my dog Buddy, and my cat Rose. I usually played alone because my brother was much older than I, and there were no other children in our neighborhood. My imagination kept me occupied from sun up to sun down. Between the swing my dad made for me in between two perfectly positioned trees in the backyard, our basketball court, my fifty Barbie dolls and stuffed animals, my blue Tonka truck, and my pets, I was all right! My solitude taught me how to use my imagination, and play alone contently. I loved my hometown and was looking forward to moving back.

The first few days back were quite bazaar to say the least. We entered a Wal-Mart and noticed the store was out of shopping carts up front. My mother and I knew that this would be a larger shopping trip since we had just moved in, so it was imperative we use one. We stopped a nearby sales associate and asked if she happened to have seen any. She grinned and directed us to the grocery section. We followed her, and she stopped abruptly once spotting one, "There ya go, ma'am, there's a buggy right there!" My mother smiled and thanked her.

She proceeded to push the cart, and I'm thinking "Buggy?" I waited until the sales associate was far enough in the distance and I asked, "Why did she call this a 'buggy'?" My mother is no stranger to southern slang and idioms, she simply explained, that "buggy" is often a word used in place of shopping cart. I'm thinking, okay, I need to take mental notes of this.

It also amazed me how friendly people were and how many people knew my mom! I mean, we just moved back here! Every time we got out of the car, there was a "Hey there", a "How's it going" or a welcoming wave! In New York, a smile is the most a stranger would give you. After the countless times of asking my mom "Who's that?" I was let down. Come to find out, none of these people knew my mom! These were only their expressions of southern hospitality. Interesting, I thought. Moving back to my hometown wouldn't be so bad after all.

After enrolling me in school, my mom immediately researched the music program. I played the trombone at my previous elementary school in New York so my mother knew that placing something familiar back into my life, such as music, would allow for an easier transition. She was right. I loved music! Although I missed my old band members, it was time to make new friends... right?

The band directors weren't much like my old band director, for some reason, they were intimidating. I could tell they took the music very seriously, and that this would be a game of skill, rather than a game of thrill but I was up for the challenge. I was given a small white slip of paper numbered one through three. From there I was supposed to inform the music department of which instruments I would like to play in order of importance.

I was new and just a day or so late with registration so I missed the day in which the music students were able to try out all the instruments and get first dibs on the ones they gravitated towards. Still not letting that get me down, I was eager to try a new instrument and be a member of the band.

I began to listen as a woman named instruments from a sheet of paper. For as long as I can remember, versatility has been important to me, so I knew I did not want to go back to the trombone. It was time for something new. As the woman was naming off instruments, I was in my own world. I tuned her out, as I did to many teachers. All I could hear was murmuring as I daydreamed. I thought back to the movie, *Drumline*. I admired the passion that those actors exuded with their musical connection to those drums. I also thought back to my grandfather and his soul band. There were so many powerful instruments in that group. Horns. Horns are all that I can think of. I got emotional thinking of his passing and the time we bonded over jazz music. I did not need the teacher to list anything else. My daydream was over, "Umm! Thank you, I think I know what my top three are." Very antsy, and anxious to go home, I quickly jotted down three words on that small slip of paper. I can still remember the list to this day. Line one I recorded "Trumpet", line two I wrote "Percussion", and on line three I concluded with "Saxophone."

Orientation was over; the weekend had passed, and before I knew it, it was time for the first day of school to begin. I was so excited to hold my new instrument, or jam out with my new set of drumsticks! The day moved slowly, but eventually, all of my core classes were over, and it was time for band class. I was so excited to get down to that band room. I think I ran to band class! (If that visual screams "nerdy" to you, you are on the right track.) I arrived to class and pulled myself together; and by "pull myself together" I mean, "controlled my breathing and heart rate from all the running." I tugged on my cross shoulder laptop bag and chose a seat at the far end of the room closest to the window. I was not really in the mood to make new friends on this day; I was anxious to see which of my three instrument choices I would be a proud owner of. Would I be an awesome girl percussionist, keeping up with all the guys? Would I be a bold, strong trumpet player? What about a smooth saxophone player like my grandfather?

Everyone in the classroom was handed small black boxes, including me. The students began to open them and attempted to put the strange contraption together without instruction. I was thinking, "What is this?" At this point, I had convinced myself that I was in the wrong class, because they handed me an instrument that I was totally unfamiliar with. So now it was time to break my silence, I tapped the girl next to me and asked, "Excuse me, what is this?" with much confusion. She examined me with arrogance, "It's a clarinet." and quickly finished putting hers together. "You have got to be kidding me," I thought. I had no idea what this dainty instrument was. "What sound does a *clarinet* make?" are among my many thoughts and concerns.

To say the least, I was heartbroken. The music department totally overlooked what I had requested. They weren't remotely close. There was a purpose for the instruments I chose. I was quite reserved and a bit shy, so this was my time to shine. I wanted to have a voice, a strong voice, and a LOUD voice and I was given a *clarinet?*

So here we are in a room full of perceivably snobby students that I didn't know, with an instrument I was completely unfamiliar with. I was in the freaking twilight zone. What was a girl to do? I am sure I could have complained to a teacher and could have possibly gotten my way by switching instruments, but that was so not me. I could have simply quit the band, as did almost half of the other students, however, I was no quitter. Once I'm signed up, I will see it to the end. So it looks like "dainty unfamiliar instrument with stuck-up classmates" it is.

As the social anxiety reached unbearable levels, I crawled tightly into my shell and began searching for ways to make myself happy. Middle school was a weird time for me. Even though I was born in Tennessee, and I did spend a few years of my childhood years here, I was still the "new" student. Making friends was a challenge. But I decided that I wouldn't let it bother me. I knew I was a good person and friends would come naturally. This just meant more time to adjust in my academics, and to perfect my musical craft.

Time went on, and I was well adjusted to my schedule and did really well in my classes. My outlook on this new school began to change and I made a new friend! We met in gym class and to my surprise, she was a clarinetist! I guess all those weeks sitting in the back corner of the band classroom, amongst my own thoughts, really did a good job of blocking people out. She and I shared similar humor and outlook on popularity; we did not care, we just wanted to have a good time, laughing and sharing inside jokes. She made my life in the band a whole lot less painful.

After many weeks of getting familiar with how to set the instrument up, learning how to care for the instrument, and gaining an understanding of which key indicated which note, we all felt quite accommodated. Those were tedious times for me. For some reason, I did not come equipped with patience for going over the same "C, D,E,F, and G" scale. I would take the instrument home and play the scale backward out of boredom. The next thing I know, the band director is teaching us to play the scale backward! As we were being introduced to new scales each day, all the students were playing them backward and forwards, and my ears were literally tired of hearing the same notes over and over again. I would take my clarinet home and make up my own songs before I even learned where all the notes were. Then, I would mimic the melodies from songs I heard on the radio. It was just fun for me! Pretty soon, it was time for sheet music. Finally!

Each week we were introduced to a new song. Oh my goodness, this was like heaven for me. Allowing notes to form melodies to make music, I was captivated. I grew fond of the art form, and I respected it. Deep down, I knew I was excelling musically amongst my peers. However, this was something I wanted to keep to myself. I just wanted to be normal and have fun times with my new best friend and enjoy being a pre-teen.

When I arrived at school in the mornings, there was time for breakfast and morning assembly before we were all dismissed to our classes. However, I never ate breakfast at school. Although I was slowly beginning to make new friends, there was still much social anxiety that came with being in the lunch room with so many students. There weren't many teachers present during breakfast, so it was way too unstructured for me. Instead of being social in the mornings, I opted for practicing my instrument in the band room. I was so thankful that they allowed the band kids to come in before classes started in the mornings and practice. The band room saved me. So at this point, I was practicing both before and after school. Initially, this dedication came from the pure love of music and interest in my newfound hobby. However, after the countless compliments from my mother and the positive feedback from my band director, I began to think, "Hey, I might be pretty good at this!" I grew obsessed with the tone, sound, and pitch of each note I produced. I had to get it right. It had to be *perfect*, and it was.

Time had passed, and the clarinet had become my life. One day, my band director announced that there would be "chair tryouts" coming up. I did not initially care about these tryouts, all I wanted to do was be good at what I did and sit next to my best friend. Then I found out what these chair tryouts were for. It determined where you would be sitting in band class. This is where things got real. I honestly had no clue where I would be sitting in relation to my best friend after these tryouts.

Well, the tryouts began, and I sat in a room with the band director's back towards me so he did not know who I was, and I played whatever scale or random sheet of music that sat in front of me. The tryouts went on all week. As the other students seemed stressed about the whole thing; I soon began to grow anxious about it as well. I think I did pretty okay in the tryout. Well, Friday came, and I found out that I landed myself in "first chair"! If you are not familiar, the first chair is the highest ranking for the most skilled player in their section. I was very excited about this. It made me feel good to know that all my excess practice paid off. My best friend was a great musician as well! She was second chair, so we weren't far from one another. We continued to sit right beside each other. Everything was going extremely well!

Happily ever after, right? Not quite. Things changed once my best friend was challenged and lost. She was demoted to third chair. So I now had a new friendly neighbor in second chair. Well, things weren't so friendly with each week. Every Friday I would look at the challenge list and knew I was going to be challenged by her. For weeks at a time she could not beat me. I practiced much harder than I did before, but this time, my purpose was different. I wasn't doing it for the right reasons. There was a severe fear of failure that consumed me. I did not want to lose, so I exercised my talents two or three times daily. It was as important to me, as homework or studying for a big test.

I had become obsessed with sustaining my title, and it simply was not fun for me anymore. This was a mental game that I no longer wanted to be a part of. Towards the middle of the year, I was challenged and finally lost. I am not sure if I lost purposely, or if I just lost the drive it took to be "perfect". I was drained. Believe it or not, I was RELIEVED! I was the happiest I had been in a very long time. The obsession with being perfect had weighed me down. The battle was over, and boy, was I glad.

Although it did take a bit of time for music to be fun for me again, it eventually was! I soon played for the enjoyment of it all not because I wanted to be the best at it or to keep a title. I played because of the bond that my grandfather and I shared. I played because of the way it made me feel. I played because of the love of it all. My goal was no longer perfection, but passion.

A new and oddly unexpected passion was gained through this as well. Remember the three instruments that I preferred to play? Neither of those instruments was the clarinet. In fact, I had never heard of one before the very day that it was placed in my hands. A tad bit of faith mixed with an immense love of music, and I ended up being really good at it, and a contender to my classmates.

Sometimes we have this "perfect" idea of how we want our lives to turn out. I envisioned myself either with a bold and brassy instrument or as a percussionist and ended up with an instrument in the woodwind family. I found out the versatility of the instrument and became enthralled with it. If I wanted to be loud like a trumpet, I controlled and adjusted my breathing to do so. If I wanted to be soulful like a saxophone, I most definitely could. After throwing a few flat notes in the mix, the jazz club would be calling in any minute. Even if I wanted to hit hard notes and rhythms like a drum, I could just by controlling my tongue and wind effort. Triplet, triplet, triplet, yes! I can keep up with the percussion section too!

You may have an idea of how you want things to go. If these things don't go as planned, that may not be the direction that is for you at that present time. Trust the direction that you are being led. God may have something else in store for you. There may be a specific assignment he wants you on right now. Why did He redirect my path musically? Who knows, maybe he wanted me to meet my best friend. Maybe there was something special that needed to happen that year that I am unaware of. The Most High is the only one who has knowledge of this purpose-driven action, and I must say, I am very happy that it happened the way it did.

In closing, do not let perfection be your obsession! Life is much easier when you live easy going. Do things simply for the joy and the passion of it all. I am not telling you not to live life determined or as an overachiever; however, it is very important to pay attention to our intentions. Why am I doing this? Is my heart in the right place? Am I happy? Be authentic and realistic in your actions and success will follow! Just remember that God can change your reality as long as you have faith. Be good to yourself in the process.

Perfection "Makeup Tips"

💋 Be mindful of your intentions in all things you do.

💋 If the plan changes from the original vision in your mind, don't freak out. This is where you seek confirmation from the Lord. If this is where He wants you, take the new path.

💋 It's okay to make mistakes, and it is okay if you aren't the "best" at something, as long as you try your best.

Mirror Moment

What specific areas in my life am I seeking perfection over happiness?

Foundation

Every Girl Needs a Good Foundation.
What's Yours?

Have you ever tried building a house without a foundation? Okay, so you might not be a carpenter. Well, do you enjoy desserts? How would you like it if I baked a cake for you and handed it to you without a cake holder or any form of plastic ware? Your initial reaction would be obvious; this cake lady is crazy. Yet, before you can fully formulate your next thought, there it is, your cake is in pieces all over the floor... dessert anyone?

As you know, we all have separate journeys, but one thing remains the same, we each face some form of adversity at one point or another. Life is filled with its many surprises, both pleasant and unpleasant; throughout it all, you must have a foundation. Adversity is indeed inevitable, so when the road gets rough who or what is seeing you through? For me, it is *who.* In my decision-making, through difficult circumstances, happy moments, times of confusion, and so much more I've made it a priority to follow Psalm 121, and looked to the Lord for my help. Christ stands at the forefront of my life and is my firm foundation. There is so much peace that comes with knowing He will be a constant comforter and helping hand for His children.

How do I know this? No matter how far you've strayed from the path you were on, Christ never stopped calling you back home, and He will continue to do so. Never will He leave or forsake you.

So let's think back to our cake. The dessert I baked you may have been pretty delicious, and I probably decorated and dressed it up beautifully. However, we were missing the single, most important element of all, its foundation.

Similarly, when we wake up, shower and dress ourselves from head to toe, looking good and smelling even better, we should not leave our sacred place before taking the time to reflect on what grounds us. Lest we forget to pray or reflect on virtues, or even recite a helpful quote or "rule" your parents gave you to go by, you are opening up the door for destruction and confusion. This all can result from a lack of guidance. In my experience, when we continue to live without being grounded, we will find ourselves miserable. Life without a foundation of some sort can very well result in a life in shambles, just like our cake crumbles on the floor.

In my walk, I have found that there are a few steps taken to assure Christ is the leader of my life. First and foremost, I needed to accept Christ as my Lord and Savior. Acknowledging that He died for our sins, builds that greater understanding of His love for us. You also want to establish a genuine relationship through prayer and devotional reading, and commit to daily authentic conversations with the Lord.

If you feel it in your heart to commit your life to Christ or would like to re-dedicate yourself to Him, begin by acknowledging Jesus Christ as your Lord and Savior, and confess the following,

'That if thou shalt confess with thy mouth the Lord Jesus, and shalt believe in thine heart that God hath raised from the dead, though shalt be saved. For with the heart man believeth unto righteousness; and with the mouth confession is made unto salvation." (Romans 10:9-10)

The combination of both prayer and devotional time is a very powerful thing. Growing up, many of us were guided to pray before we eat, or my personal favorite, saying prayers before bed. Bedtime prayers have always brought me peace.

As we grow older, the practice of prayer often becomes something traditional and routine. Recently, I attended a women's prayer conference at my church and was reminded the importance of prayer. It's not just something you do out of tradition or habit, it's so much more than that. Prayer is a time to humbly give thanks and appreciation to the Creator, it is a time for conversation between you both, and it is a time for peace.

Additionally, always remember to be specific in your prayers. If you have been experiencing negativity in the workplace or with a coworker, be specific, ask God for protection and peace each day before you enter. Sometimes we have financial strains. You may be in college and did not receive enough aid or did not quite get the refund you were expecting to pay for your housing. Finances have been hanging over your head, but you only want to focus on school. Be specific, "Lord, I come humbly to you in my time of need. I am asking for a major financial breakthrough in my life right now. I also thank you in advance for the strength you will provide me to get through this situation."

I struggled with devotional time growing up. It was always hard for me to sit still and take in information for long periods of time. Tedious Bible study sessions made me view Bible reading as something unobtainable, or a practice I would understand more, as I got older. This does not have to be the case.

Bible reading can be fun! Your daily devotional time does not have to feel like a chore. Besides, this is a sacred time for thanksgiving and peace. As soon as I changed my mindset, and began believing that fact, I became much more consistent with this special time of the day.

Devotional time can be described as spending time with God through reading the Bible, and other related Christian literature, and through prayer. Why is it important? Incorporating time for devotional into your daily life strengthens your relationship and personal connection with the Lord. He desires a close relationship with us! As your relationship grows deeper, so will your "...peace which passeth all understanding..." (Philippians 4:7).

Each of our schedules, personalities, and relationships with God are different, so it is important that you try a few different strategies and figure out what works best for you. If you are a morning person, this may be the best time for devotion for you. If you are the opposite, try having devotional time mid-day or before bed. Whatever you do, try to create a fundamental pattern for yourself. Here are some basic tips and suggestions to assist you in creating daily devotional moments just for you!

1. Create a quiet environment

For me, my quiet place has always been my bedroom. This may be different for you. You may enjoy sitting outside on your porch while the birds chirp and the wind blows. Or you may prefer this time at your desk at work or out in your car during a lunch break. Wherever you are, be sure to avoid distractions. Power off your television, cell phone, and put away your laptop. You want to be fully invested in your study and prayer time.

2. Open and close your devotional time with prayer

Be sure to begin and end your devotional time with prayer. You can begin by simply asking God to open your heart and mind to receive the information He would like for you to receive. Close with thanks and seek assistance from Him to help you follow the path He would like for you to take. Again, this is for you, so include in the prayer whatever you need to include; I am only giving suggestions to guide you through the process.

3. Make connections

Be sure to connect what you've read with the topics and concerns we deal with each day. Apply your biblical knowledge to your situations and allow your skills to grow stronger with each day.

4. Be prepared

This is study time! Just like school, you come prepared with pencils, highlighters, notebooks, your textbook, etc. You will do the same thing with devotional time. Have your Bible, or whichever form of Christian literature you use. Definitely, have a notebook or journal for your devotional time. You want to record Bible verses and notes to have for reference later.

Make your devotional time fun for yourself! Get colorful notebooks, pens, and markers. Involve your friends and family and do fun weekly challenges. For example, each week you can have a memory scripture. By the end of the week, each participant of the challenge should have the scripture memorized. Or, you and your family can play Bible trivia. This does not have to be a dull and tedious time for you.

Whatever your foundation is, be sure to keep yourself knowledgeable and grounded within it. Life is filled with surprises. It is important to be mentally and spiritually prepared for war each day. You don't want to end up like our cake!

'For other foundation can no man lay than that is laid, which is Jesus Christ.' (1 Corinthians 3:11)

Jesus, I Need You

Hey Dad, I need you

I cannot do this on my own

I will look to you for my help

And your sacred place will be my home

Agape

Your love is greater than any mountain

Wider than any sea

The highest form of affection

And the standard for what genuine love should be

You are the light of my life

Creator of all creation

For Jesus is the light

And the ruler of the nation

All of my problems, all of my fears

I submit them all to thee

I do not have to bare it all

For greater is He who lives within me

Live Without Worry

'Be careful for nothing; but in every thing by prayer and supplication with thanksgiving let your requests be made known unto God. And the peace of God, which passeth all understanding, shall keep your hearts and minds through Christ Jesus.' (Philippians 4:6-7)

At the tender age of eight, my grandmother wrote a very special scripture (Proverbs 3:5-6) down for me onto a piece of scrap paper, and I never forgot it. "Stop worrying!" She exclaimed, with a voice of reason and a means to an end. My thoughts were along the lines of "If only it could be THAT easy". It amazes me that at such a young age, the amount of anxiety that consumed me. What could bring a child anxiety, and what was I worrying about?

Obviously, I am no stranger to apprehension. This was a struggle for me from childhood up until, well now. I am still learning how to cope with anxiety. I remember going through a breakup and the thoughts of losing my companion to someone else circulated my mind regularly. I am also reminded of a time I was unsure of whether or not to quit a job in which I was unhappy, questions and "what ifs" consumed my thoughts, and circulated through my head. Situations like these physically made me tired.

In the midst of distress, I would justify the anxiety by concluding I was only "sorting through my thoughts." However, the reality of it is, if these thoughts are causing you pain, there is no just reason. The Bible says, "Peace I live with you, my peace I give to you; not as the world gives do I give to you. Let not your heart be troubled, neither let it be afraid." (John 14:27).

Worry and anxiety are very real and active feelings. The act of agonizing or constantly dwelling over life's misfortunes is not only unpleasant, but it is also a very draining thing to experience. You do not have to go through this.

God does not wish pain or hard times on His children. He wants us to live peacefully, and without fear. Do not worry about the "what ifs." Pray about your troubles, and leave them alone. Trust that the Higher Power will handle it for you.

So if you find yourself in a painful situation, remove yourself and seek refuge in the comfort of the Lord. If you are wondering how this comfort can be reached, read the word and apply what it says to your life. Pray and plead with him, and then let it go! Continuing to dwell decreases your faith. Enlarge and restore your territory by trusting that your Heavenly Father will handle it all for you.

Seek the help of the Lord. Lean on Him, because you cannot do this alone. The battle is not yours to take on. "Trust in the Lord with your heart and lean not on your own understanding." (Proverbs 3:5) Unload all of your problems, doubts, fears, and give them all to him! Lastly, in your conversations with our Heavenly Father, let him know of your burdens.

Ask God exactly what it is you would like Him to do. Be specific in your talks with the Most High. If you are unsure of someone you are currently dating, ask, "Lord, please reveal to me whether or not YOU want this person in my life." Or if you are struggling with a career decision, be direct and express to Him what you need, "Lord, please provide me with direction and the answers I need regarding my career."

It is important that you trust in the Most High that your uncertainties will be handled. Worrying causes personal setbacks. You only gather unwanted energy and fret, which can slow your thinking and vitality. Keep your positive energy high, and remove worry from your life.

Mirror Moment

What concerns in my daily life worry me?

Mustard Seed

'And Jesus said unto them, Because of your unbelief for verily I say unto you, if ye have faith as a grain of mustard seed, ye shall say unto this mountain, remove hence to yonder place; and it shall remove; and nothing shall be impossible unto you.' (Matthew 17:20)

I remember it like it was yesterday. I was a sophomore in high school, and it was Wednesday evening at church. I loved going to church after school because when you are the last to leave the nest, things are pretty lonely at home, so the more time I got to spend with my peers, the better.

I loved my friends, my church, and all of my youth pastors. We were silly and cut up in church quite a bit, but every once in a while, miracles would happen. On one sweet day, my miracle happened.

My youth pastor's wife sat us all down to share her lesson with us. On this particular day, I was really tired and wanted to go home. I was not at all interested in what she had to say, but my thoughts were along the lines of, "Okay, I'm here so let's get the show on the road."

As she was talking, she began to pull a few items out of a grocery store bag that she had on the table. Something that appeared to be a spice for a seasoning, "what is this lady doing!" I am still very tired, and still anxious to go home, but I'm listening.

She spoke softly, "Jesus says, if you have faith small as this mustard seed, anything is possible." My jaded disposition faded as I studied the seed. You could barely see it. If you aren't familiar with what mustard seeds look like, take a quick moment and look it up. They are very tiny.

As I processed the lesson, I felt a sense of peace and optimism. Wow. God promises if we could just have a very small amount of faith, just as tiny as that mustard seed, He would make mountains move for us! Amazing. I never forgot that lesson. I was younger then, so the lesson had a much greater impact in my life later on. In those dark seasons, I would picture that mustard seed, and meditate prayerfully with the mere faithfulness that God would pull me through, and He has time after time, as He will for you.

There will be times where your back is against the wall, and mentally you may feel trapped. This may feel like the end. However, do not let this notion deceive you! This is the trick of the enemy. Things are going to look really bad but you'll have to believe in the things you can't see, just as you believe in the things you know to be true. These are moments when you need to put on your temporary blinders and walk through the thorn bushes until you feel the soft roses again. 'For we walk by faith, not by sight.' (2 Corinthians 5:7).

My friend, I am here to tell you if you just have a minuscule piece of belief that God will turn your situation around, He will! It has happened for me. I am reminded of a time when I felt low. I sought counsel from a family member, and they kicked me while I was down. I had very little strength to move on, but I had a glimpse of faith that I would not be down for long. That was all I needed. I said a simple prayer, as lay in bed and gazed up at the ceiling. With a soft and spiritless voice, I asked The

Lord to "order my steps." 'Order my steps in thy word: and let not any iniquity have dominion over me.' (Psalm 119: 133). Literally hours later, my situation turned completely around! The mistake came with me trying to do it all on my own. Be still, turn your problems over to the Most High, and believe that it is already fixed. Let go and let God!

It is that divine faith that will push you through those obstacles. It does not matter how big it is or how often it occurs; but if only for a moment you have faith as tiny as a mustard seed, you can spark the light of your future. How do I know I have faith? Faith is that thought in your mind that says, "You know what? I have really had a terrible day today but I know things will turn around eventually." Or specifically, "I am very sick today, but it is comforting to know that eventually, I will be myself again. I will get better soon. I always get better. Jesus always heals me."

Be still and very quiet, this is not a time to search for answers; this is a time to cling on tightly to hope. Remember, the teacher is always quiet during the test. Grab on to those whispering thoughts of positivity in the back of your mind amongst that negative situation. Hold on tight. 'For his anger endureth but a moment; in his favour is life: weeping may endure for a night, but joy cometh in the morning.' (Psalm 30:5)

Mirror Moment

In what areas in my life do I need mustard seed faith?

Mustard-Seed Faith
"Makeup Tips"

- You only need a minuscule amount of faith to know that God will handle your situation.

- Belief comes by reading the word of God, and having knowledge of these capabilities.

- Do not faint in the face of adversity, instead, keep pressing on!

Eyeliner and Mascara

For Those Eye Opening Moments

At one point or another, we all will have some profound eye-opening moments come our way. Although these moments can be quite alarming, they are often valuable in the aspect of revealing necessary information to us. This information can be useful.

What insight did I gain from this? How can I apply this lesson to my life moving forward? Keep reading as I show you the power of those valuable eye-opening moments.

Wait... I'm Black?

You would think a child playing at daycare would be filled with fun and innocence right? Not necessarily. My entire life changed when I discovered I was BLACK. Okay, so this was not actually the discovery of my race. But, one sweet day, amongst the merriment of kids laughing and the sweet sound of nursery rhymes, I was reminded of the obvious.

"You can't play with us; you're black." Instantly, my hopeful heart, eager to make awesome friends at this new daycare was altered. My perception about making friends and myself changed. "I can't play with them because I am black? What's wrong with being black?" Quite honestly, I didn't even pay attention to her being white or having blonde hair or blue eyes or a gray dress. These details made no difference to me. I just wanted to make friends. This is honestly the moment when I felt the innocence and purity of life seep away from me. Geez. I had more fun at home playing with my Barbie dolls, stuffed animals, and "My Little Pony". I should mention that my Barbie dolls were all colors of the rainbow.

I was introduced to the idea of segregation from a classmate who was more than likely taught this ideology at home. This was not her error. Nope. This indeed is a product of role modeling. Somebody she looked up to showed her the differences between the color of another person's skin in comparison to hers. Not only did they show her the difference, but they also gave her a lesson in value. She was taught that her value was much greater than one with a dark complexion.

It was the very concept of value that prompted the child to turn me away from the group. As I turned away, my eyes opened to the hatefulness that the people of this world are capable of. I did not hate her; she enlightened me. Although her words and actions were painful, I learned something new.

The little girl's words opened my eyes to racial opposition. However, the beauty of that hurtful moment was priceless. I went home tearfully and expressed to my mother the details of the unfortunate occurrence, and with a calm disposition and a smile, she prepared to repair the pieces of my emotions, "Black is beautiful, and you are beautiful just the way you are." Here is where I began to love and embrace who I am. I wanted to learn even more about my ethnicity, and why "Black was beautiful." I love and have pride for who I am, and where I come from. We all should! In having pride in our cultures, we should also love and embrace other cultures.

Our external differences should not make us take a second look at one another. We all have a heartbeat, and we all were created equal. When we focus on viewing others as souls, instead of placing importance on outward appearances then we will have truly practiced the art of love.

Empty Journal Entries

To this day, I am still unsure why I did this. I can tell you now that I would love to hug and comfort my younger self, "Your words matter. I want to hear what you have to say."

I remember my first diary. At the tender age of seven, I swelled with pride over this new landmark that I was about to embark on in life. Okay, don't laugh, it really wasn't a *diary* in journal form. It was more like an index card, or a sticky note. Yes! That's it; it was a yellow sticky note. I hid the note from my mother, enclosed with the name of my first crush, and stuck it in a popcorn tin. "Mom, you CAN NOT look at my diary," I exclaimed (with the hopes that she actually would). So, of course, my mother did not quite know it yet, but she was pretty much my best friend, and I was ready to chat with her about my first crush!

Now, I only did this because all the cool teenage girls I watched on TV hid their diaries from their parents and their annoying siblings, so I wanted to do it too! Obviously, I got in waaaay too much TV as a child. Anyway, I was only in first grade when I proudly hid my "diary" from my mom. This was my very first occurrence with journaling.

After a while, I grew to love journaling! I had many different journals, with fun colors and prints. I even had one with a lock on it which was my absolute favorite because it reminded me of those teenage girls on those shows that I was telling you about before. Yes, I was in heaven.

The realization came as a young adult, as I was going through my old things, I realized that I had kept a journal or two from my childhood, but I tore out the pages. My initial thought was, why isn't anything written in here? Then I quickly remembered that I was not so sure about the quality of poetry and did not want to look back later on my thoughts, and feel... embarrassed. This was a major eye-opening moment for me. I was ashamed by my work because I lacked the confidence and self-assurance of my capabilities. Reflecting on this to this day still breaks my heart.

If I could, I would hug my younger self, and let her know, "Your words and thoughts DO matter. You are brilliant and creative; I would love to read this!" I have recently begun journaling again, and I have made up for lost time! So if you do not take away anything else from this book, please journal. No matter what age you are or what capabilities you may possess, your words matter.

Journaling is fantastic! The sheer fact that you only need a pen and pad to sift through your thoughts is golden. The therapeutic benefits of journaling are wonderful as well. Sometimes we just need to talk it out and if you are like me, and need to talk but have no one to talk to at the present time, write it down. I want to highlight a few benefits of journaling, and then end with some journaling tips I have picked up along the way.

Benefits of journaling:

1. **The ability to allow yourself an emotional release**

   This is your time to release your inner thoughts and feelings. No one is judging you. Misspell words, scribble on the page, scream, do what you need to do to let it out!

2. **Reduce stress, and more effectively solve problems**

   Writing out situations gives us the ability to analyze them carefully from a different perspective.

3. **Reflection**

   With journals, you have the ability to look back and reflect on your past situations. This is a time for praise reports! Looking back at previous journal entries allows you to say, "Hey, I overcame this, and this is how!"

Journaling Tips:

1. **Be Consistent**

   Whatever your personal journaling goals are, try to be consistent with those. If you would like to journal once weekly, stick to this! The easiest way to do so is by setting aside a certain day for journaling. This makes it much easier for you to remember and keeps you aware that, "This is my journaling day." If you are a daily "journal-er", stick to a specific time for your journaling. It may be easy for you to journal each night at 9:30 p.m. before bedtime. Pick what works for you and be consistent!

2. **Keep it with you**

   You never know when you may need to quickly get your thoughts down. Carry it around with you to capture when you're inspired.

3. **Date and title each journal entry**

   Dating your journal entries is extremely important!
   When you reflect on previous entries, dates give you
   a timeline of your life. This timeline gives you a visual
   to see how far you've come, and possibly what steps
   you've taken to get here.

4. **Do not limit yourself**

   These are your words. The only person who needs to
   see them is you. So do not be afraid to lay it all out
   there. If you are feeling pretty crummy today, say it!
   If you want to write in all capital letters, DO IT! If you
   feel like scribbling all over the page, and simply
   adding a date at the top right of the page to signify
   your emotions for that day, then, by all means, have
   at it. This is your personal space.

   Hopefully, these tips become beneficial to you
moving forward. If you do not have a journal, look no
further! Throughout this book, I have equipped you with
a journal pages to get started. If you are new to journaling
or want to start back journaling, the pages I have
provided will give you the practice necessary to start
your journey. Jot down the thoughts and feelings that you
may be experiencing as you read this text and get into the
habit of bringing alive those emotions.

   The missing journal entries from my adolescence
showed the doubt and uncertainty I felt regarding my
capabilities. This has been eye-opening for me and has
reminded me of the importance of accepting and valuing
one's skills and capabilities. We should embrace the
skills we have because they are special. No one else can
do what you do the way you do it.

You may not think you are the best at something but with time and dedication, your skills improve, and you will reach your personal goals and potential. The multiple journals I have currently, the poetry I share with you in this book, and my growing love for creative writing shows that I overcame those doubts and have accepted my talents. This year, I even had the courage to perform an original spoken word piece for the talent portion in a pageant. I will share it with you at the end of the book!

Accept yourself through the uncertainty. Embrace your uniqueness. Beat out those gnawing doubts!

Mirror Moment

What am I failing to accept about myself?
(What are YOUR "missing journal
entries"?)

Body Image

Each and every one of us has a body image. It is completely natural for humans to have some form of perception regarding the way we look. The important question is: do you view yourself and your body in a positive or negative light? Hold on to that thought, and answer that question after we highlight some key areas of what body image is. According to GoodTherapy.org, body image includes a mental picture of one's physical body and one's attitude toward the physical self. In essence, it is how you view yourself, and the thoughts and feelings that are the product of that self-image.

One's body image, however, does have the ability to change over time. This shift is often due to social, cultural, or familial interactions. Some of you may be thinking, "Family! How can my family alter the way I view my body?" Well, there are many ways in which this can indeed be possible.

"Looks like you have gained weight!" What better way to be greeted on a summer visit to a long-distance family member, right? Not exactly. Has an older family member ever commented on your weight? Has the concern of "Am I too fat or too skinny?" consumed your thoughts growing up?

In my experience, many of the older women in my life have struggled with weight gain so there is a gnawing pain there that just won't ease up. Elders have a tendency to speak their minds anyway, so combining this with their own fears of weight gain, and their concern for your health; painful comments may be an end result in efforts to help. That grandmother, great aunt, or whoever it is may not mean any harm; they might even have helpful intentions; but what they do not realize is that by commenting on the weight of a growing child, they are creating a complex for a future adult. That person has now opened up the potential for long-term negative effects.

I am reminded of carefree summers; cool, wet grass beneath my feet from a nearby overflowing water hose, pool parties, and barbecues with endless food. Not once in this segment of my childhood did the daunting thoughts of feeling too heavy or any related thought enslaved me. My innocence carried power here, and it was sweet.

On the contrary, there are those following summer years as I grew with the trees and gained awareness that I did not look like the other girls. I grew anxious over beach trips because I hated the fact that my friends and classmates could wear two-piece bathing suits and I had to opt for the one piece or shorts and tank top combination. Well, my mother never liked those two-pieces on young girls anyway, but that's beside the point. When did this change occur? And what was the catalyst for this change?

The shift in my personal body image could have been the cause of a number of things; mean comments from classmates, emulated behaviors from those around me, or society's lack of realistic images of women in the media in general. Luckily, we are now seeing more realistic images of women in the media, but there could be more.

My point is, not one person or instance is to blame. The goal is to change our mindsets. Remember when you were a little girl with no concern for how you were viewed based on your appearance? You wore your favorite shirt twice in a week, not because you didn't have options, but because it was the lime green *Rugrat's* shirt and it was your favorite. You were more satisfied with what made you happy. Let's get back there. We know innocence does not last forever, but it is okay to channel that inner child-like carefree mentality.

The only concern regarding our bodies we should have is making sure we remain as healthy as possible. Prove you love and appreciate your temple by making healthy food decisions and living an active lifestyle. 'What? Know ye not that your body is the temple of the Holy Ghost which is in you, which ye have of God, and ye are not your own? For ye are bought with a price: therefore, glorify God in your body and in your spirit, which are God's.' (1 Corinthians 6:19-20).

We are made special, and we are to treat our gifts as the sacred sanctuaries that they are. Let's change our mindsets and make better food choices in order to feel better and live longer.

If you have developed a body complex, it does not have to stay with you. Practice self-love. Your body is your temporary home, so let's love and enjoy the time we are spending in it! Take a look in the mirror, and make this declaration: "I am beautiful, just the way I Am."

Mirror Moment

Have I been practicing self-love in regard to the way I view my body? In what ways can I achieve this goal?

Blush

Things That Make Us Blush

Dating

My most memorable date was a picnic at the park with sub sandwiches and a shared bag of hot Cheetos. Seriously! We had a blast. It was simple, thoughtful, and we both had a really great time exchanging unadulterated laughs with one another.

I am thankful for the "traditional" date experiences that I have had. You know the kind, when the date knocks on the door for you, opens the car door and lets you in, opens the restaurant door, pays for your food, and takes you back home. I enjoyed myself on those dates, and have felt very respected and appreciated as a woman.

Traditional dates are still very much needed. But the appealing part of the picnic date for me was the simple and carefree aspect of that evening. Not to mention the attention to detail by picking out my favorite bag of chips. That was a plus.

If you haven't already, once you've reached dating age and are ready to date, you should simply begin to focus on actually being friends with whomever it is you are interested in. Don't concentrate on having a boyfriend. Just because you and a guy have great chemistry and similar interests; it doesn't warrant that you two should rush and begin a relationship. Dating should be a fun time amongst two friends!

Eyebrows should raise if you find that you are being pressured or coerced to move too quickly in any aspect. I was always warned by my dad, uncles and other male figures in my life to watch out for these signs. But even when we are warned, we always think we are an exception to the rule. "I won't experience that. Those things won't happen to me." Well, as soon as I began dating I saw and even experienced exactly what they were talking about. One moment, you have just had your very first phone conversation and then on the next occasion, he calls you "baby," tries to make physical passes, or tries to even kiss you. Does that even add up? If you are just getting to know someone what type of feelings could be produced in that short amount of time?

If you aren't ready for these things, don't allow them. Remember, no means no. It's your body, and at the end of the day, you have control over it. Don't allow anyone the power to persuade you to do things you aren't emotionally prepared for. In my experience, this only opened the door for romantic expectations to follow that I honestly, just wasn't ready for.

Dating should be a fun time! You want to laugh, exchange views, discover common interests, and participate in fun activities with one another. The stress and mental strain that comes with trying to decipher whether someone is into you for the right reasons just isn't worth it. You want to be sure that your dating experience is as jovial and as stress-free, just as the dynamic with your close friends could be. Focus on friendship, and love will follow.

Fall in love with yourself before allowing someone else to love you. The only way to do this is by making you your number one priority. Take care of yourself. Get pedicures, not because you want to be perfect from head to toe for that potential date, but because it gives you that warm and fuzzy feeling on the inside after doing something good for yourself. Cook for yourself and learn what makes your belly sing. Be good to yourself first! Eventually, you'll learn your requirements and desires in a mate that will compliment you pleasantly.

Ladies, it's not the outward search for love, but the inward search. Let love find you and in the meantime, master the art of loving yourself. To someone, you are an answered blessing.

Dating "Makeup Tips"

💋 You should not at all feel pressured to do or feel anything you are not ready for.

💋 Dating should be fun, and does not require physical or romantic involvement.

💋 Fall in love with yourself before allowing someone else the opportunity to do so.

Mirror Moment

In what ways can I love myself in the meantime? What are some self-care activities that I can take part in?

Saying Goodbye

After coming to terms with my reality, things got easier.

And once I took power over the truth, its intimidation withered.

I finally accepted the fact that he wasn't the one, and that's okay.

It was beautiful, it was ugly, and it was a love story.

The book is closed, and there is a much greater story to tell.

I will love again, and the withered flowers will bloom.

There will be a Happily Ever After.

It matters not, why he doesn't love you as you love him. What matters is why you don't love yourself enough to walk away.

Breakups

Who would have thought that a major breakup would bring so much gain? Yes, I said "gain" and not pain! No pain no gain right? Oh, the joy of breakups. I could not have completed this book without discussing breakups. Boy, did breakups give my mind a run for its money.

My first actual breakup was pretty bad; I mean it hurt baaaad. Devastation is the only word that I can think of at the present time to describe my initial reaction to him and me parting ways. I had just cut my hair because I did not want to continue chemically treating it and I wanted to start over and grow my hair out naturally. I always had very long hair, so cutting it was completely new to me, and on top of that, it was a short, curly afro! New territory for me, but I did not care, I was ready for the change, and I loved it! I did not think that I would have been having issues within my relationship in the midst of all of this. This was my long-time boyfriend and after years of love and friendship, we parted ways.

I took a second look in the mirror the day he left me and started questioning myself. Am I not pretty enough? Have I gained weight? It's my hair; yes, it's my hair! Directing all the attention on my appearances, turning aspects of myself that I once viewed as beautiful into flaws, when in reality, he and I had been having issues for quite some time.

Rejection is among the most complicated feelings we experience after a breakup. Rejection likes to make you feel as though you aren't good enough. Some of us don't like to face that possibility and challenge rejection for a re-match. Round two, three, or seventeen has now become a matter of proving your self-worth. How many rounds will you go before letting go? If your value isn't seen here, then it is simply time to walk away. This doesn't mean you have failed; this means you have found the strength to move on.

The psychological wounds created from being rejected from someone I once loved and trusted stung for long time. As I mentioned previously, I blamed myself for the breakup; this magnified my misery. Understand that our response to romantic rejections is usually finding imperfection in ourselves.

Frankly, breakups are caused mainly due to mutual differences. Sometimes, things only happen for a season. Seasons change. The leaves always wither, and the snow always clears. Pointing the finger at yourself and justifying the breakup because "you weren't pretty enough" or because you "didn't love hard enough" only kicks you while you're down. You are already experiencing pain from the breakup, don't hurt yourself further by blaming yourself for the demise of the relationship. You are beautiful, and you gave it your best try.

It's vital that you know who you are and the value you carry. If you have been rejected from a relationship, that's fine. It was not destined for you two to be together, or your worth was not fully seen from this person. If he hasn't already, one day, the right person will see the full value you possess and take you off the shelf before anyone else does. The important thing here is, do YOU see that value? The confidence and self-assurance you have within yourself will show on the price tag. You want to be as appealing as fine china for your future mate. Eventually, you will be off the market for the right person, for good!

I lost a boyfriend, but I gained myself again. The tears I cried during the breakup, used to equate to an endless pain from someone I missed. After surviving the heartache, I look at tears so much differently now. Crying is okay because the sun always comes after the rain. It rained for many days and many weeks during that awful time for me, but I smiled again. I laughed again. I dated again. And most importantly, I loved myself again!

I experienced a new strength, with this breakup. I loved on myself stronger than I ever had before. I threw myself in the gym, not because I wanted to lose weight, but because this was my way of blowing off steam and taking control of my body and independence. I clung to God tighter than ever before because He was the only source of my strength. What did you learn from your experience? If no one else has told you, you are strong for getting through this, and you are definitely worthy.

Mirror Moment

What have I gained as a result of rejection?

What I needed was inside me all along.
This strength gave me the power to move on.

"Love is like a mask"

Love is like a mask

The truth hides behind superficial walls

Spectators are unsure of what is real

And just like a mask

There is often mystery in what we feel

Love is like a mask

When unveiled, it is often enlightening,

Alarming, and sometimes frightening

Funny thing about masks,

And your ability to remove them

There are two faces

Two realities

Real and unreal

Pleasure, pain

Love is like a mask

Highlight

Areas of Life We Often Wish to Highlight

Social Media
"All that glisters is not gold"
~William Shakespeare~

We live in a world where technology is the leading component for communication. You have a party coming up? No need to mail out invites, just Facebook invite your friends or send or an E-vite, and they will be there. What about those long distance family members who can't make last minute travel plans for your recital? Just live stream the event, they won't miss a thing! Technology has become the answer for most all of our problems, but I can admit that there are times where I wish things were classic and that technology wasn't such a huge deal.

Just today I had a few things to send out in the mail and felt the biggest joy in going to the post office. What a nice change. Now do not get me wrong, there are many benefits of technology. However, there are those classic moments outside of the normal electronic dependency that are simply refreshing for me.

The gift that our advances in technology have given us is social media. Social networking sites have completely taken this world by storm. Just about everything, is posted and documented. Emphasis on "just about." Not all things are documented, of course.

On most social media outlets, we see a general trend in which users highlight the most positive aspects of their lives. You know, the exciting job promotions, the graduations, the vacations, proposals, and other related accomplishments. All these things are beautiful, but what about what you *don't* see? Like the job terminations, the failed classes, the breakups and even the divorces. What about these things? I question this, not because I want people to post these adversities, but to bring some reality into what we see on the Internet. Contrary to what you may see on the online, people are going through hard times, just like you! Social media is a highlight reel, you don't see the process, you only see the final result. You don't know what goes on behind the scenes. You more than likely will not see these types of things broadcasted.

Just now, I stopped what I was doing and decided to take a quick Facebook poll of my own. My objective: begin at the "Home" page; scroll down while counting each personal post. Stop counting once you reach a "transparent", non-glossy, or non-celebratory post. My result: I scrolled past a total of twenty-three inspirational, celebratory, and humorous posts until I finally reached a post that was transparent.

In reality, many of the issues that we do not wish to post or share are private to us, and we are dealing with those things on our own. So, of course, we are not likely to post them. I totally understand that.

The important thing to take from this is to be very careful in how you react emotionally to what you see online. Steer clear of comparing your life to others. Everybody is going through something, and there's always adversity in the shadows of success, which we usually don't see. It isn't just you. You are not alone. So before you log on to your social media, be prepared to know that it is likely most of your friends will be posting the upsides to their lives. This is, of course, a time to be happy for your friends; however, do not compare this to where you currently are in life.

Many of your peers may appear to be doing well, and because their job or opportunity seems greater than yours, you may feel that you are not doing as well as you could be. Be gentle with yourself, you are doing the best you can. Your personal achievements should not be measured by the likes of others. Instead, hold yourself to your own realistic standards. Do not hold yourself to someone else's standards because that is not your life! God has his own path for you and only you. When you abide in your calling, there is no need to be competitive. Besides, what fun is it having the exact same goals and path as someone else? Make your own path. If your friend or colleague's path is straight, zig-zag yours! It's okay!

One of my mentors does this awesome thing where she posts a status, inviting users to share truthfully how his or her day went, good or bad. I love that! We are all human, and we all have bad days. Sometimes it feels good to know that we aren't alone!

I also wanted you all to be aware of not only how you respond emotionally to social media, but also how you use it. Matthew 6:1 says, 'Take heed that ye do not your alms before men, to be seen of them: otherwise ye have no reward of your Father which is in heaven.' (Matthew 6:1). Whatever righteous, charitable, or philanthropic endeavor you may take on, do these things simply with a pursuit to bless those that need you.

Be mindful of posting or sharing your acts of kindness at every chance you get. This is, of course, fine, if it is done in moderation, or for informative purposes. Maybe you want your friends to know different ways they can feed a family this Thanksgiving. That would be great information to pass along! However, for the most part, God wants the wonderful charitable acts we do for others to be done in private. It is not necessary for those things to be displayed at every chance, allow your actions and the way you treat people to speak for itself! The only one that knows your heart is the Most High, and His opinion is the only one that matters!

All in all, remember to be happy in whatever stage you may be in life. Do not let social media or other forms of technology rule your thoughts. Celebrate achievements like sticking to your workout plan, discovering a new hobby or rekindling an old hobby, committing yourself to journaling, traveling to a place you've never been before, saving, and all things that make you smile!

Social Media "Makeup Tips"

💋 You have done, and are already doing amazing things; do not compare your life to others!

💋 Be mindful of how you respond emotionally to what you see, because "All that glitters isn't gold."

💋 Celebrate your own personal achievements.

Mirror Moment

In what areas do I compare myself to others? What steps will I take moving forward to change my mindset?

Accolades and Accomplishments

Growing up, my parents never pressured me to do well. Remember, I was the girl who faked not being sick when I actually was to get out of staying home from school. I still have no clue why I did that. Doing well academically was always important to me.

I never really understood why my mom was so laid back regarding my performance in school. I always heard my peers discuss getting rewarded for their good grades. I even saw kids on T.V. get cash rewards from their parents for good report cards. "Five bucks for every A? That's easy enough; I get all A's anyway!" I remember living in New York in the third grade, and I got my very first report card of the year. "Mom, Mom, look! All A's." I was hoping that she would share my excitement because I mean, we did move to an entirely different state, and I did need to adjust to new ways of learning and new teachers and of course, I wanted five bucks for every "A", just like I saw on T.V. Her response did not surprise me. "Good!" She said only. I froze, in my mind, I'm screaming at myself "Sharonda! Remind her about that T.V. show with the kid... and, and the money and the report card! Tell her!" But all I could do was stand there.

It was not until last year that I finally asked my mom, "Why didn't you or dad ever pressure me to do well?" I also wanted to know why they didn't make it rain money on me when it was report card time, but I left that part out. "Because it was expected for you to do well." Quite honestly, I already knew this answer. I knew there was an understood expectation that I pursue academic excellence, but I wanted to know why. Why did you guys expect this? How did we get here?

Either way, I had become pretty much obsessed with academic accomplishments. I do not know when this started, but I do know that I have always sought approval through my academic achievements for as long as I remember. Like, if there was an award for coming out of the womb the best, I probably had one. Right now, in my mother's memory chest, there are awards and trophies from my brother and me overflowing in the chest. Perfect attendance, award banquets, spelling bees, band awards, it didn't matter I loved it all! I needed it, like an *obsession*.

Since becoming aware of this obsession, I began to analyze, why exactly did I seek validation through accolades and accomplishments? This could have been a longing for bigger praise and recognition from my parents or maybe I just equated overall happiness or success to doing well in school. It could be a combination of both, and if I could be quite transparent, I do not know the answer to this question. But what I do know is, that seeking validation through accolades is not a healthy thing for the brain. What happens when you don't win? Then how would you feel about yourself?

Growing up my life was full of awards and ceremonies, then as soon as I entered college, reality hit. You are just another student fighting for greatness. Yes, I received awards in college, but I was one of many. When the recognition slowed down, things got real for me. There was a point in time where I felt like an absolute loser as if all that I was striving for was just not enough. I wanted to be the best at it all.

Eventually, I got tired of seeking validation from my accolades and accomplishments and began living for myself. Those "highlighted" areas of my life no longer defined who I was. It wasn't until I made the personal decision to be in charge of my happiness, that I finally broke that way of thinking. I continued to do my best, but this time, I didn't wait for the applause.

I clapped for myself and sought inward joy and acceptance. This was when the real happiness entered my life again. Your awards and prestige do not measure success, but the peace you achieve each day, and the people you impact along the way, these things are what make you successful. Speak this declaration:

"I do not need validation from the opinions of others. What matters most is how I feel about myself."

Accolades "Makeup Tips"

👄 Do not seek validation from your accolades, accomplishments and those "highlighted" areas of your life.

👄 Titles and awards do not define you! Who you are on the inside defines you.

👄 Take charge of your emotions, and chose happiness.

👄 Don't wait for the applause of others, clap for yourself!

Mirror Moment

*What areas in my life, do I seek
validation? In what ways can I change
this way of thinking?*

Lipstick

For Those Finishing Touches

Confidence

"Whether you come from a council estate or a country estate, your success will be determined by your own confidence and fortitude." – Michelle Obama

What does confidence look like to you? Is it shoulders back, chin up, bright eyes, and an even brighter smile? Is it a strong model walk? Or is it more of an elegant, but powerful saunter? Is it loud speaking or is it more of a direct and unfaltering tone? Maybe when you think of confidence, there is a certain person you have in mind. Begin to formulate what confidence looks like for you, and keep that in mind.

Life is about evolution. Remember before you wore lipstick there was lip-gloss. There was growth and indeed maturity that needed to take place before appropriately wearing this beauty product.

Confidence is the same way. We were not necessarily born with the skills and tools to be completely self-confident. We had to come about this on our own. Unfortunately, moments of discomfort and often sadness have taken place, which have forced us to develop tough skin. We may have been broken down in the process, but eventually, we learned what it took to build ourselves back up.

The "nice girl" had to have been written on my forehead as a child. I loved to smile and wanted to see everyone happy. This carried on with me...well until this day. It's a part of who I am. However, I had to realize that some people are hurting and that hurt sometimes causes people to be plain mean. These were the people that often took my kindness for granted. As I grew in my confidence, I had to realize that it is okay to smile and be kind to people. However, you still have to let them know what you stand for and what you will not tolerate. When you are kindhearted, people often make attempts to take advantage of you. If you have a kind disposition, always remember to have dignity and possess the courage necessary to stick up for yourself.

I still have a ways to go in my journey, as we are all constantly growing; however, at this present time, I feel the most self-assured. Confidence, for me, came with time, year after year, pain after pain, and lesson after lesson. I grew smarter and most importantly, I grew stronger. All the things that I have gone through have attributed to this confidence. Do not despise your hardships. Every trial and set back that you experience will attribute to your personal growth.

As you are on your confidence journey, beware of the "A word". Acceptance is the dangerous word to look out for. The need for acceptance will come at you right and left. Be aware of what it is and the potential harm it can bring. Whether you acknowledge the existence of social circles or not, you know if you or your friends are accepted into the "cool crowd." What matters here is how you feel about yourself as a result of this. Then there's the time for college. Whether you decide to attend or not, everyone knows the pressure that comes with "getting accepted into college."

We desire acceptance from our peers. You grow older and wish to be selected or accepted into organizations or social groups. But what happens when you don't get selected? How do you feel about yourself? The likely answer to this question is rejected. If you take these things hard, remind yourself of whom you are and who you were before this. Before the rejection, you held your head high with optimism for life, so continue to do so! Keep moving forward.

The important thing to know here is that the only entity you should strive for acceptance from is Christ Jesus. As you navigate through life, the true power you receive will not be from acceptance into social circles or groups; the power will come through accepting yourself! There is completeness in this feeling. Striving for accepting from others, and often failing may leave you feeling incomplete.

The road to self-confidence is not the smoothest of roads. It comes with many bumps, detours, and roadblocks. It is often the road less traveled. Are you ready for the ride?

As I mentioned in chapter one, we are His clay and God is the potter. 'But the very hairs of your head are all numbered.' (Matthew 10:30) 'For thou hast possessed my reins: thou hast covered me in my mother's womb. I will praise thee; for I am fearfully and wonderfully made: marvelous are thy works; and that my soul knoweth right well.' (Psalm 139:13-14)

What does "fearfully and wonderfully made" mean? You may hear many people use this term. You may see it on graduation caps, T-shirts, photo captions, etc. But what does this really mean? Well, let's break it down.

Fearfully, means to have reverence for God's creation. He has individually crafted us and with much care; therefore, we should appreciate His love and take the best of care of our temples. We should have a deep respect for our homes and be mindful of what we allow to enter into our bodies and our minds, for we should honor Him accordingly for this precious gift.

Wonderfully, each and every one of us has been made special. Out of the seven billion people in the world, no one is like you. From your unique fingerprints to your internal organs, you are made distinct. You are unlike anything else. Isn't that special? Not only did He make you special, but He also has a plan and special purpose just for you! 'For we are his workmanship, created in Christ Jesus unto good works, which God hath before ordained that we should walk in them.' (Ephesians 2:10) Hold your head up high and walk with purpose in everything you do!

For brevity, we are worth something to God so we should feel worth something to ourselves. Love yourself from head to toe, and inside out. Know that you have a purpose in being here, and let that very thought be your motivator. Let your light shine, and don't allow anything or anyone to dim this light.

Again I ask, what does confidence look like to you? Whatever you see as self-confidence, you can achieve. This is obtainable. You have a special and unique purpose and are beautiful in every way.

Also, remember that true beauty comes from above and begins on the inside. Who are you? Are you a good person? What is the nature of your heart? Allow these things to illuminate from the inside out.

You are amazing, and I pray you see this for yourself. Your beauty will show by knowing how God sees you and loves you. If you don't feel accepted, take comfort in knowing that God already has accepted you.

Mirror Moment

What does confidence look like to me, and

what steps do I need to take to reach it?

Love yourself,

Genuinely and utterly fall in love with self.

There is so much fulfillment and gratification that

comes with being comfortable in your own skin.

Grow fond and familiar with your wants, needs, and

desires

Amongst that inner intimacy should birth thankfulness

Thank God for unconditionally loving you, and be

grateful to Him for uniquely making you.

Due to the simple notion that there is no greater love for

us than His

It is an obligation and complete duty to remain in tune

with the cadence of your heart, and the rhythm of your

blood flow.

Continue to master the soundtrack of your life.

You are a masterpiece.

Love yourself.

Coming into Your Own

"The privilege of a lifetime is being who you are." –Joseph Campbell

I want you to know; it will get easier. Pretty soon the worries of the world will fall off of your shoulders. The things that used to bother you or even devastate you won't even play a part in your life. There's a little thing called resilience, and you are capable of mastering this art form.

How will you get here? Wisdom. Wisdom is reached through your ever-growing experiences. These experiences, though often difficult, shape who you are. With each encounter, each tear, each heartbreak and heartache, you will learn and you will mold beautifully. You will gain knowledge and advice to share with your family and friends.

Look at the trees. See how they stand tall and strong? They have seen the sun switch with the moon. They have withstood the windstorms only to lose a few branches. They have felt the heaviness of the rain and experienced the power with each lightning strike. The deafening roar of the thunder in all its might, this could not intimidate those trees. It still stands in all its beauty. It continues to grow, give, and love. Just like you.

Through all that you have been through, you have survived. If you feel like you can't get through a tough situation, look at how far you have already come! Keep going, and keep growing. Remember, God won't give you more than you can bear. You can do this!

"I accept only positive, healthy thoughts and feelings of myself into my mind."

"The key to success is to keep growing in all areas of life-mental, emotional, spiritual, as well as physical." -Julius Erving

Reflection (A Performance Piece)

When?

When will you smile again? But mean it.

You said you would put yourself first. But do you
believe it?

When will you stop contemplating death, when you
deserve to live?

And when will you realize that you are enough, when it
feels like you just don't matter?

The search for perfection... when will you learn to love
your reflection?

What will it take?

TRULY forgive your father for his mistakes,

TRULY forgive that boyfriend who reminds you of an

absent father who left you, and a love that won't accept
you.

I know he left you, but Jesus kept you.

Your healing can be done, but easier said,

When led by your emotions and not the creator of all.

But God tells you to cast your cares upon him,

And he will never let the righteous fall.

And I'm here to tell you, it once was me...

Because at seventeen I had low self-esteem

And suffered a depression, so deep

I contemplated suicide...

But I am here today, and living out my dreams!

Although the road isn't easy

Each day I put God first,

Instead of breathing my last breaths

I chose to breathe LIFE into others.

Today I am a woman.

Adjectives to associate with me are fearless and free.

Now when you look in the mirror what do you see?

When I see my reflection, I love myself, for real;

Because I am the girl that allowed herself to heal.

"Happiness is the secret to all beauty; there is no beauty that is attractive without happiness." – Christian Dior

Connect with Sharonda

To contact Sharonda Stiggers for speaking engagements, please send an email to info@sharondastiggers.com

For words of encouragement, continued offers, virtual discussions, and much more subscribe to: www.sharondastiggers.com to hear more from the author.

"Like" Sharonda Stiggers' Books on Facebook for quick updates, and weekly motivation!

Stay connected with Sharonda! For business, social inquiries, or more information connect via email, Facebook and Instagram!

Remember to review my book on Amazon.com!

Made in the USA
Columbia, SC
29 July 2023

20903421R10083